To En
Li'th

Xau

The first book that Jean Can
RUFUS THE NEW FOREST ᴵᵁ̅ᴵ̅ᴵ̅, ᵖᵘ̅ᵇ̅ᴵ̅
Frederick Warne. For a number of years she contributed articles for country magazines, including subjects such as skiing, riding, shooting, gardening, and the economics of the countryside. She has also written books on a number of specialised subjects. More recently she has returned to writing on the countryside with PINE TREES AND THE SKY, an account of her life in a cottage in the Cairngorms in Scotland, where she brought up her son, Hugh. Their first dog in the cottage was a Labrador called Cocoa. When she arrived, two-year-old Hugh could say three words, cheese, car and cocoa. Therefore the dog was called Cocoa and every dog afterwards has been called after a drink. Thus Sherry became Sherry. The term Herself used in the book, to denote ownership, comes from the Highlands.

SHERRY

Jean Cantlie Stewart.

SHERRY

THE AUTOBIOGRAPHY
OF A SPRINGER SPANIEL

JEAN CANTLIE STEWART

Cover and Frontispiece by Andrew Lawson Johnston
Drawings by Heather O. Catchpole

ROWAN BOOKS
KEITH, BANFFSHIRE

By the same author

Rufus the New Forest Pony
The Writing on the Blackboard
The Quality of Mercy
Why Devolution
History and Practice of the Law of Mines and Minerals
The Sea our Heritage
Pine Trees and the Sky

First published 2005
Copyright
© Jean Cantlie Stewart

ISBN 0 9509932 5 5

Typeset by Tradespools, Frome, Somerset
Printed and bound by Antony Rowe Ltd., Chippenham, Wiltshire

Contents

Acknowledgements

I am indebted to my two illustrators, Andrew Lawson Johnston for his excellent oil painting of Sherry, which we have used on the cover of the book and also as a frontispiece in black and white, and Heather O. Catchpole, whose skilful and delightful drawings have brought the text to life. I would also like to thank Amanda Reid, who, with her husband David, called in unexpectedly on their way home from holiday in the West and took the true-to-life photographs of Sherry, which were of benefit to both illustrators.

I also thank all the kind friends who supported the publication of this book, particularly Prue Kennard, who, on her own initiative, marked the typescript up for illustration, Jennifer and Donald Phillips, who introduced me to Heather Catchpole, and Emma Snowball, my enthusiastic eleven-year-old editor, who suggested some useful cuts. I also for the second time in my writing career thank the children of St. Thomas Primary School, Fulham, who listened to my reading the book with genuine interest and helped me with their criticisms.

CHAPTER I

A Happy Family

I am an old dog now and before I get older or more forgetful I would like to tell you the story of my life, because I think it would help you to understand how we dogs and Springer Spaniels in particular think and behave. My name is Sherry and my markings are liver and white. My nose is liver, surrounded by a white ring. My head is liver and so are my ears. I have a large white ruff round my neck, which runs to the centre of my back, where I have a liver saddle and more liver in a patch near my tail and four furry white feet. People say that we Springers, so-called because we can jump high, are much smaller than we used to be, which means we may have been crossed with another breed many generations back - perhaps, who knows, a small Sheep-dog. Occasionally I meet a large old-fashioned Springer and look up at him in awe. Big or small we are all good hunters and dash into undergrowth to put up game and rabbits, our floppy woolly ears protecting the sensitive hearing parts from thorns and burrs. We work mainly by smell and like to go ahead of people, sectioning the ground in search of scent. People say we are difficult to train and we think this is because we are too intelligent and independent, although those who do not understand us think we are stupid. We know better. Ours is a good club, and, if I see a member of the Spaniel family anywhere, I go and talk to him in preference to other dogs.

I was born of Scottish parents fifteen years ago in the stable of an old manse in a green glen in Perthshire, with fruit trees surrounding a lawn in a walled garden and the sound of water gurgling over the mossy stones of a Lowland burn. I had 5 brothers and 4 sisters and before we opened our eyes we made a wriggling mass of liver and white silkiness, pushing and shoving against our long suffering mother in order to be fed with her milk and kept warm by her body. We lived in a large wooden-sided box and before we opened our eyes we staggered blindly about on uncertain legs among the crackly gold straw which was changed daily. When our eyes opened and we could see we tried to clamber over the sides of the box and our fat tummies and short legs must have made us look ridiculous as we straddled the top. Soon, once down on the level again, we were exploring the wide stone-flagged passages and stalls of our timber and stone stable. It was summer and the weather was warm, so soon we were allowed out into a gravel yard and later (when there was a member of the family to keep an eye on us) onto the sunlit lawn in front of the house. Just picture 10 fat liver and white silky puppies exploring the outer world for the first time - it was a dream time of happiness for us all.

To puppies people are extensions of their families. There were two adults in our household and three children, who came often to the stable, first to feed us and then to pick us up, stroking and cuddling us. We gave them lots of warm licks in return for their love and kindness and when they were with us we were much more adventurous. On one occasion we got into trouble. Men came to paint the outside of the house and there were lots of pots full of white stuff lying about. One of my brothers had a completely brown face, which we teased him about, so perhaps he wanted to be more like the rest of us, who had white on our faces. Seeing his opportunity he buried the whole of his nose, right up to his eyes in one of the pots of white paint. He looked really funny and he made us laugh, but

what a job it was for the children to get him clean. It was also very uncomfortable for him to be scrubbed so hard with spirit and water. On another occasion when we were in the garden we got a bad fright. If there was no one to watch us we were put into a high wire pen. When someone came to feed us we stood on our hind legs trying and failing to scale the top of the wire netting in anticipation of our meal. One afternoon three huge machines in the sky flew over us very low, making a horrible screaming noise so that we were petrified and all managed to clamber over the wire and run as fast as our little legs would carry us back to our kennel. We never succeeded in climbing out again, although we were growing bigger all the time.

I secretly thought I was the prettiest of all the puppies and indeed people constantly said so. But when strangers came to see us and choose a puppy to take away they always chose one of my brothers or sisters. Perhaps this was because I had a funny nervous habit of making little dribbles along the ground whenever I was admired and thought I was going to be picked up. I did not understand the reason for it and the more I worried about it the more it happened. The result was that people took away another puppy and never me. By this time of course we were all weaned, which meant we did not take milk from our mother any more, but lapped it from a big bowl which had crunchy cereals in it. One day a lady, who had seen us before and chosen one of my sisters but then changed her mind, because she said she had not time to have a puppy, came back to see us again. By now I was the only girl left and apparently that

was what she wanted, so she picked me up and carried me to the
the grass in front of the house. "That puppy won't lack for
love", said a family friend. I decided she was the one I would
like to go away with and that was how it turned out.

It is a shock for puppies to leave their home and their mother
and brothers and sisters and the family of people they know and
suddenly to be on their own in a new home they do not know.
People do not realise how great is our sense of loss or how
overwhelming the anxiety that we feel at this time. With all
arrangements made I was suddenly placed inside something that
seemed not unlike our box in the stable, except there was no
straw and it was moving fast. I was in fact in the front of a car in
the place where people normally put their feet and my tummy
did not like swinging round corners. Soon I was sick and we
had to stop the car and get out. I was not house trained either. I
tried to sleep, but could not and I began to miss my mother and
my brothers and sisters, so I clambered up on the seat and then
on to my mistress' lap, where I kept wanting to be cuddled. But
she was turning the steering wheel this way and that and did
not have much time for me. I know now of course that when
the car is moving it is the driver who makes it go and keeps it
on the road. I have learnt also that one must not unduly distract
the attention of the driver because if you do, he or she may
make a mistake or not notice someone else's mistake and the
car will stop suddenly, throwing you forward which means you
hit your head on the windscreen. So, since I have grown up, I
am careful that, although sitting in the front seat which I like to
do, I am not a nuisance any more.

After a drive, disturbed in this way, we arrived in another lovely garden. Here there was a big white gate and old stone garage at the top of a gravel drive, which, lined by thick shrubbery, led down to the front of the house and then continued round it to the back, making a circle. I soon found that the drive was just long and steep enough for me to get up a bit of speed and this became one of my favourite things to do. Every time we left the car in the old stone garage by the gate I rushed down to the front door and then on round to the back, with my ears flapping up and down in the excitement of my run. This garden was full of undergrowth and how I loved it! It had more flower beds than the one I knew in the place where I was born, and there were wonderful rabbit smells underneath all the plants. I would often disappear to sniff these scents, and, because no one could exactly spot where I was hiding, I was able to take no notice of people shouting for me, as I hid under the great broad leaves of the herbaceous flowers. There was a fence round the garden with wire netting. It prevented me jumping out, but the rabbits knew their way through from the wood. Because of this and because I could not easily be found in the shrubbery and foliage, my strongest animal instinct, hunting for rabbits and pheasants, could be exploited to the full.

CHAPTER II

How I Was Nearly Sent Back in Disgrace

Although I loved my new home I quickly got myself into serious trouble which might have affected my whole life. I had two bad habits. The first I have told you about and it was still troubling me.

"Don't draw attention to it", a friendly dog trainer said and she was right. The moment I stopped worrying about it I began to stop leaving a little trail of water when people spoke to me.

The second fault was more serious, because it made people very angry. The moment I was shut in by myself I howled and sang and tore everything apart with my teeth - either at night or when I was left in the house by myself during the day. Perhaps coming from such a large family I was frightened to be alone. It was incredible the amount of damage I could inflict on a room - I tore up the floor coverings and ripped into the doors with my teeth and claws. The more I gave way to the panic the more panic-stricken I became. I was terrified of being shut in and alone and the fear fed upon itself. It was like something bursting in my brain. People do not agree about what it is that makes puppies do such things. I am sure that if I had had another dog to talk to I would not have done it. But all I had were constant reminders about the two Labradors, aunt and nephew, who had used the big wicker basket that was my bed and I was repeatedly told that they never did such things. Some friends that came to the house said that it was because we as puppies had had too much happiness, too much cuddling from an early age, which had made us too demanding. But when I met my mother and my brother and sister again I could see they did not behave like that and they thought I was very silly. Maybe I was born anxious and always expecting disaster – or perhaps I was sufficiently spoilt to think that my demands would always be met. That is not a good lesson for children or puppies, but I will tell you a secret – most of my demands in life have been met, and by getting my own way in a number of things I have managed to keep my phobias at bay and consequently have had a very happy life.

Although there was no other dog in my new home I soon made friends with the New Forest pony, Rufus, who taught

me a salutary lesson. Herself lifted me up in her arms and Rufus and I touched noses. He had soft nostrils and he enjoyed blowing through them and snuffling my nose. I liked that, but I also liked chasing him up from the back when he was being led and herding him through the gate as if I had been a Sheep-dog.

"Do not do that", I was told sharply. "He will kick you".

Springer Spaniels, however, are very bossy and I was convinced, as we usually are, that I knew best and that it was safe and sensible for me to be in charge of the operation - seeing that Rufus went into his field properly. I even sometimes pulled his tail with my teeth when he was going through the gate. Then one day with no warning he quietly raised one shod hind foot and bowled me clean over, squealing with fright. He did not kick and I was not hurt, but that finished that game. I learnt my lesson and I understood not to get too close to his heels when we went riding. At first this was only in the field behind the house, because puppies should not be walked out in the first few months of life, but should exercise themselves. The field offered limitless opportunities for smelling and hunting, for it was full of the scents of rabbits and field mice, all of whose underground homes required excavating. Then, as I became older and stronger, we began riding through the beech woods, where there were carpets of bluebells in early summer. On these occasions I had no time for my own ploys, because I had to keep up with Rufus as he trotted and cantered, and I was anxious that if I got left behind I might get lost.

But I am going on too fast - first I must finish telling you about how I was nearly sent home in disgrace on account of my refusal to be shut up on my own even for a few minutes. I did not chew things, I demolished them, cushions, books, spectacles, floor coverings, sponges. Nothing,

absolutely nothing was safe from my sharp little teeth. Whenever I was shut in my initial annoyance and fright at my confinement quickly turned into blind terror that I might be left there indefinitely on my own. I was no longer in possession of myself. Nothing was safe from the destructive force of my phobia. Herself is a very busy person - I realise that now and try to help her to keep up with her work. So within a few weeks she began to despair of my strange habits.

Luckily for me, however, I had made a very understanding friend in my new home. Sandy came to help most days in the garden. He seemed to understand my phobia and when they were having coffee and the conversation turned to my transgressions I could hear him taking my side.

"I've never had a puppy like this before", Herself would say, "neither of the Labradors behaved in this way. Sherry can't even sleep on her own in the kitchen, let alone stay for an hour or so while I'm out. I lead too busy a life to compete with her hysteria. I'll speak to my friends on the telephone. I think she'll have to go back".

Each time she said this Sandy talked her out of it, but one day there came a crisis. They shut me up for a short time while they went to fetch something in the car. They knew how much I loved being in the car. Why had they not taken me too? I was very annoyed and by the time they returned my annoyance had again turned to panic and I had gone beserk. The kitchen looked as if there had been a terrible accident. Everything was torn, broken and destroyed. Herself was downright and definite in her tone of voice.

"That's the end," she said, "I've already spoken to my friends. I can't stand this a moment longer. She goes back tomorrow".

Sandy remained cool and calm as he always did. "Unless," he said, "you give her another fortnight".

Puppies do not have large vocabularies. Dogs cannot speak, except with the expression of their eyes and by the movement of their tails, but as they get older they understand many words, because of the association of these words with things and actions. They also understand tone. On this occasion I picked up enough of the sense of the conversation from its tone and from the few words that I had by now understood. I didn't know what a fortnight meant, but I realised this was my last chance. Either I made a big effort to become a good dog or this would not be my home much longer. How could I cure these panics? I realised I must trust people when they said they would return and I began to listen carefully when they said, "Be good and I'll be back soon". "Back soon" became the key words. It meant they would be returning shortly if only I had the patience and the trust to wait. So, whenever the panic began to increase I told myself repeatedly that I must trust them - they would not let me stay too long by myself. I loved these people. I thought of the house now as my home. So there and then I decided I would make a really big effort to grow up.

At the same time Herself made a difference in my routine. She knew how much I loved cars. Even as a tiny puppy I would be happy sitting in the car by myself, watching people passing by in the street, so instead of leaving me in the house I went with her always in the car and was happy just sitting there while she went shopping or did her other business. I knew that she would always return to the car and meanwhile I was not alone, there were so many things to distract my attention. Also, if I had to be left alone for a moment or two in the house, she would leave her coat with me, the coat she wore every day, so that I knew she could not go away for a long time without it. But I have never forgotten that I owed my whole happy future to Sandy. When we moved house up to the north of Scotland I went back to stay with him from time to time and lay in front of the fire with his cat. When I was there he taught me to carry my own lead, which was a very useful habit, and even when I tore up a piece of his floor covering when he left me on my own for a short time he was not really cross. He always saw things from my point of view. He was a good man and he was my friend.

CHAPTER III

The Country Mouse Becomes a Town Mouse

By now I was used to travelling long distances in the car. If I wanted to see the road I sat in the front and if I wanted to sleep or if the car was going at what I thought was too fast a speed I sat in the back or on the floor under the dashboard. When sitting on the front seat the world was laid out before me - rabbits scuttling off the tarmac, pheasants proudly strutting across the road as if they had all the time in the world and later - when we moved to the Highlands - grouse getting up out of the heather calling 'Go back, Go back'. There were people, lorries, horses, cars and in the distance fields, hills and trees. The only thing you could not do in the car was smell the scents that you knew were out there beyond the glass.

One day the car was loaded with suitcases and we went on travelling for hours. As evening fell we came to a curious place. It was different from anything that I had ever seen before. There were no woods, hills, fields or animals, although here and there among the houses there were great stretches of grass and trees called parks, where squirrels lived. Otherwise there were just streets and more streets and cars, red buses, bicycles and people. At first I was bewildered, but I soon began to like the men and women that I met in the street, because so many stopped and patted me and said how beautiful I was. Being, as I have told you, a little pleased with my appearance, that suited me very well and so I began going up to them and wagging my tail, asking to be made a fuss of. Because Sandy had taught me

to carry my lead and because, as time went by, I became more adventurous, I was able to walk ahead on my own and turn round to greet the people coming along behind. They were almost all of them happy to talk to me and give me a pat and tell me how clever I was.

At the beginning of my stay in this strange place, however, I was not clever at all and was lucky not to have been killed in the first few weeks. In one of the parks, with Herself not noticing until too late, I strayed for a second on to a cycle track. The next moment a racing bicycle with a man on it with his head down, quite unable to see, and with no bell to alert passers-by, hit me amidships and rolled me over and over squealing with fright and pain. At first I thought I had been killed or permanently disabled, but then I found to my surprise that all my limbs worked and that I was only shocked. From that moment onwards I learnt to listen to certain warning words and my vocabulary increased. 'Car' could mean our car, but in a different tone it meant a warning; 'bicycle' was a warning; so also was 'look out' and 'wait'. With things in this place going so fast there was not time to be disobedient or to think you always knew best. After this unpleasant experience I understood the meaning of the command 'wait' – and so I was able, as I have told you, to go ahead safely on my own and stop when I came to the end of the pavement and had to cross a road.

This place to which we came – mostly in the winter months – was called London and I learnt, when Herself used the word, to stop thinking about digging for moles and to think instead about avoiding motorists. Perhaps the oddest thing about it was that we did not live in a house with stairs. Instead our rooms were all on one level and if you were a dog you could not see out because you were a long way up from the street and the windows therefore showed you only the sky. There were stairs in the building, but we did not even reach the flat by climbing them, although sometimes we went down, with me running ahead at great speed. Instead, you stepped into a box, the door shut behind you and you were off, going up so fast that it gave you a curious sensation in your tummy. I liked going in the lift because everyone who stepped inside spoke to me. My favourite person was a man in a wheelchair, who was always cheerful and gave me a rub behind my ears. "Where's my girl friend?" he would ask and that was me. Not far from that lift there was another one we also used, with lattice doors that you could see through. I liked it better in many ways, because I

could see the floors passing and did not feel so shut in. From our floor you could see down the shaft and so, in order to try and puzzle out how it worked, I would stand for many minutes at the top gazing down, but I confess I never fathomed the answer.

I quickly made lots of friends in the block of flats, particularly among the porters who were on duty in the hall. They talked to me as if I was a person, which I like, and they also found me balls to play with in the park. They warned us to avoid Mickey, the handsome cat, who lived in one of the ground floor flats. My feeling towards cats was mixed. I liked chasing them. So if they looked frightened and started to run away I chased them. But if they looked superior and stood their ground then I presumed that they wanted to be friendly like Sandy's cat, in which case I was either polite and left them alone or I made friends. Cats like Mickey are in a category of their own. We were warned by the head porter that he was savage with dogs, because a dog had attacked and hurt him, so we kept out of his way. Once, however, we met him unexpectedly in the courtyard, coming round the side of a car. He flew at me, spitting with rage, with his front paws outstretched and his claws out, intending to bury them in my eyes. Luckily I was on the lead and Herself shouted at Mickey and dragged me away, otherwise I would have gone for him and been terribly injured. Brave dogs do not run away. I once stood my ground with a mother stoat who attacked me and a Corgi in a friend's garden. She had a family of baby stoats, which she was defending, and I was lucky that the bite she gave me did not break the skin. After this experience with Mickey I understood that we must communicate from opposite sides of the hall. I sensed that he would have liked to make friends, but, as with all animals, memory of past experiences cannot be eradicated, except by longstanding trust.

Because I could not see out except to the sky, the fear of being shut in even for a moment, which I had suffered in the house, returned in double measure. On the first occasion I ate the whole of a large rubber sponge and had to go to the vet (or animal doctor) and have pink medicine. He had Springer Spaniels of his own, so he was not particularly surprised and he gave me chocolates, which I enjoyed. After that I was never left alone in the flat even for a second. Herself was too anxious that I might start scratching up the carpets. So I went everywhere with her in the car or on a bus or in a taxi. If it was not convenient to take me inside the building that she was visiting or working in, I would, as in the country, sit happily in the car watching the world go by. Sometimes people would come too close to the car so that I thought they were going to try to open a door, and consequently I learnt to show my teeth at once, otherwise someone might have tried to make off with the car and me inside it. The world in London is an interesting place to watch, but you have to be careful to guard your own things.

This new habit of baring my teeth had its dangers, however, because I did not differentiate between friend and foe. Therefore, when children in London - either Herself's grandchildren or friends' children - came to the flat for a meal and then took me for a walk in the park and threw balls for me, they had to be warned never to come near me in the car and it was always locked when I was inside in case they did not do what they were told. I was very fond of them - I loved playing with them and letting them take me for a walk on the lead, but the car was my territory and I dared not change this principle. Even when the grandchildren moved to the country and had a Golden Retriever of their own, I still would not allow anyone except Herself to take me out of the car, and sometimes I was quite grumpy even with her. I have heard her say to people that both the Labradors behaved in the same way, although they were not quite so fierce, and she always points out that I have to show that I can defend myself if I am sitting in the dark in a car all alone in a big city, when no one knows from whence danger may suddenly come.

CHAPTER IV

I Visit the Parks

I want to tell you now about the stretches of grass and trees in London, which are called parks, and which are like the country, except that there are no fences, cows, sheep, rabbits or pheasants, although there are grey squirrels, ducks and pigeons. The parks gave me confidence, because they made me feel at home. So when we came from the north and drove into the centre of the city we always stopped at a corner of Regents Park, in order that I could get out and run after the squirrels, who were not frightened because they knew they could escape up trees. Then we went to the flat. This routine reminded me that the grass, which seemed like the country, was never far away.

Twice a day we went to one of these parks or gardens, either in the car or on our feet. In Battersea, just over the river, I made friends with the Labradors, Sheep-dogs and smaller dogs of every kind. Of these the smartest were the Whippets in their red coats, who raced against each other and were too superior

to talk. My favourites, as I have said already, were the Springers, but there were Cocker Spaniels too and small King Charles', all members of our club and - to us - just a little different from other dogs. There are no dog fights in London parks because no one looks on the place as his or her territory. Nevertheless I regarded the Alsatians and Dobermans with some trepidation, unless their owners kept them under tight control. Once, a huge young Doberman came at me so fast that the silly girl holding the expandable lead let go and the heavy handle came flying through the air towards us so fast that the lead wrapped itself round and round Herself's legs, causing her to hobble about for many days.

In Hyde Park there were horses to look at, which reminded me of home. Sometimes they were ridden, and, beautifully brushed and dressed, they proudly trotted and cantered round the sandy track on the outside border of the park. Sometimes four of them together pulled carriages on which sat men in livery, who controlled them with long reins. Now and again we would stand and watch as men riding black horses and dressed in silver armour, with plumes on their helmets and carrying lances in their hands, practised drill on the sandy track or within a stockade built for the purpose. "That's the Household Cavalry", I was told and I was happy to sit and watch them, with the sunlight glinting on their armour and the leaves beginning to come out on the trees.

When I first arrived in London I was only a puppy, so I was not obedient, and when I was not on the lead and saw a dog I wanted to speak to I rushed off into the distance, without realising I might get lost. Once I thought I spotted a brown rabbit and streaked off at break neck speed, only to find it was a tiny lap dog, to which I had to apologise for giving it a fright. But it was nothing to the fright I received because I was suddenly all on my own surrounded by strangers until I saw Herself pounding towards me. I never got caught like that again. One day, however, when we were watching the soldiers drilling - this time accompanied by men with trumpets and drums - suddenly one of them, dressed in yellow and gold and riding a huge brown and white horse, started banging the drums, which he was carrying beside him on his horse. The drums went boom, boom, boom. As I have told you Spaniels, particularly Springers, have very sensitive hearing, so when I could not stand it any longer I decided to return to the car by myself, covering the half mile at a very fast walk with my tail between my legs. It was sensible of me this time not to run and disappear into the distance. Nevertheless Herself, frightened about the cars and bicycles on the internal roads, called and called in vain and could not keep up with me. Once I was out of earshot of those terrible drums I stopped to wait for her. Although no damage occurred as a result of my fright she spoke very severely about my show of independence. Not long after this incident we met a man from the barracks where the horses lived, and he had a very well trained Springer Spaniel of much the same colouring as myself. He carried a knotted rope which he produced from his pocket saying, "Don't be too soft with these Springers and don't be deceived by their sentimentality. They're as obstinate as mules and much much tougher than they appear. They like everything in the world to suit themselves." Herself was much stricter with me after this conversation and I began to watch my p's and q's a bit more.

There were two other gardens to which we sometimes went. In Kensington Gardens there was a Round Pond with little toy boats sailing on the water, which we stopped to watch, and ducks and geese which did not run away and squirrels which did. If you spotted a squirrel on the ground you could chase very fast and then, just as you thought the gap was narrowing, up a tree it went, clinging on with its sharp claws and laughing

at you. In the Chelsea Pensioners' gardens down by the river there was a white rabbit, to whom I used to talk. He was safe behind wire and we became very good friends. Everytime we returned to London I went to check out that he was still there and we continued our conversation from the last time we met. In that little park we always played ball. Herself would throw a soft tennis ball and I would retrieve it and give it to her, as I would have done if it had been a game bird, which had been shot or the soft sock which she threw at home. One day I got into trouble because I picked up someone's golf ball by mistake. This man in a dark blue soldier's uniform became my best friend. He was a Chelsea Pensioner and he hit the balls with a club. We had long conversations with each other, but he was not pleased about me retrieving his ball. He wanted it left where it was. I will tell you more about that incident in a later chapter.

Now I must tell you about the most frightening thing that happened to me all the time I was in London. We were in Hyde Park on a lovely sunny morning, warm enough to stop for many minutes to watch the Lifeguards trotting round within their low wooden stockade. From where I sat I could see the horses between the bars and hear the rhythmic pounding of their hooves. Suddenly there was the most terrifying explosion. Being older now than when I got the fright from the drums I knew that it was safer not to run away but to stay with Herself. She bent down to pat my head and said, "It's a bomb". I was terrified, because I had never heard any noise like it in my life and when I stood up my tail was stuck between my back legs, so that I thought I would never move it again. But the strange thing was that the horses and their riders took no notice at all. They just continued going round as though nothing had happened – even their ears did not move, they were still pointing forward, as if they were happily concentrating on the task in hand. We began to walk back to the car, and all the way I noticed that everything in the park was normal. Although my tail was so stuck between my legs that my hindquarters felt stiff, the other dogs were walking along as though they had not a care in the world. They did not look frightened and neither did their owners, who continued to stroll in the sunshine as if nothing had happened. I began to wonder if I had imagined it all. But then I remembered that Herself had been shaken also, and she had used a new danger word to me – a bomb!

As we approached the car we met, as usual, people hurrying along carrying brief-cases. They looked like the people with the dogs, just going about their business quite normally and there was I with my tail still stuck rigid between my legs. I was too unnerved to care whether I looked silly or not. There was a man in uniform standing in the car park.

"That was a bomb", Herself said to him. "Where was it?"

"Oh no", said the Traffic Warden, "That was just soldiers letting off small explosions in the barracks. They do that quite often".

"Very loud for a small explosion in the barracks", Herself replied.

When we got home she turned on the wireless and listened to a voice. Then she turned to me and used the same word again – a bomb. Someone had exploded a bomb in the car park just over the street from where we were and someone had been hurt. Later on that day we went to see my best friends who live in a mews house near the Park. (They always keep a special ball for me in a drawer in the sitting room and I go straight to it whenever we go to visit them). They talked about the bomb, and Tom explained that the horses are specially trained not to be frightened. But that did not explain the behaviour of the dogs.

"If Sherry had not been so frightened", said Herself, "I could have believed, looking at the behaviour of the other people and their horses and dogs, that I had been imagining things. Now I know what is meant by sang-froid".

Obviously sang-froid is what I need to make me more like other dogs.

CHAPTER V

Ponies

Having told you about the horses in Hyde Park, I want to tell you more about Rufus. Sandy cared for him while we were away and when we were at home I followed him everywhere and we went for rides together through the wide tracks in the woods, where the bluebells and bracken grew, walking, trotting

and cantering. If it was wet horses and walkers slipped and slid on the mud and I would have to be hosed on return to make me clean. How I hated that cold water. Some horses galloped, which we did not, and their riders made jumps on the pathways, so that the horses churned up the earth on take-off and landing and turned it into mud. All the walkers said 'Good morning' to us as we passed, but they told Herself that there was ill feeling about the condition of the muddy state of the tracks. When we were out on the road the lorries and cars were equally polite, slowing down whenever they saw us. Herself carried a crop with a long lash, which she could crack at me to make me stay in behind her and prevent me straying out on to the road. Occasionally we went to a meet of the foxhounds in the car and I saw the huntsman controlled his hounds in the same way. When the huntsman wanted to clear a way through the drivers and foot followers for himself, the hunt servants, their horses and the pack he always used the same polite words, 'Hounds, gentlemen, please'.

I used to hear Herself explaining to people why she still kept Rufus, her son's last pony. "I gave him away to friends twice", she said, " because he is really a child's pony, but he's a rebel, which is why, when he first came to us from a dealer, he was half starved and covered with fleas. Each time he went off he invented a new vice in order to come home. The first time the child had a poor seat, so he learnt to do fling bucks. He did one with me after he came home and I hit him very hard with my whip. The second time the girl could not hold him out hunting, so he took the bit between his teeth and gave her a fright".

One day, when we were going to London for a few weeks, Herself gave permission to a boy, who had been riding Rufus in the field under her instruction - while I dug for rabbits - to continue riding him in the same field. "Only there," Herself said firmly. "He will be too much for you on the road unless you have an experienced rider with you. You must not take him out on the road by yourself". But dogs are not the only beings who think they know best, and so the boy took Rufus out on the road, where he shied at things to frighten him, making them both nervous. Then he fell off and Rufus ran away and broke his bridle, so they had to confess what had happened. Rufus had always liked 'spooking' at things when we rode together, but only to make sure they were safe to be passed. Now, having got into the habit of shying, he continued to do so when Herself was riding him, despite being told off repeatedly. "Of all the many vices of a horse," she said to Sandy, "shying is the most difficult to cure. If you use a stick it makes the vice worse. I don't know what to do to stop him. I must take expert advice because it is really dangerous."

The words were barely out of her mouth when misfortune struck. She was sitting loosely in the saddle, because the doctor had allowed her to ride for the first time after she had had a swollen leg. Rufus suddenly took fright at seeing a little girl behind a hedge, who leapt off a swing and ran up and down shouting – her light frock appearing and disappearing behind a hedge of young trees. Rufus did a U turn and fled, with Herself shooting through the air, hanging on to the reins and landing with a tremendous thump on her back. She was in bad pain for months, walked with a slight stoop afterwards and did not ride again for a year. "I've been told now", she said to Sandy later, "that to prevent shying you must wear spurs and use the leg on the other side to the scary object to keep the horse going straight. I was sitting too loose".

By the time we started riding again Rufus was 27 years old and feeling his age. To look at he seemed a young pony, but he went slower now and liked to turn for home earlier than before, which – because he was a senior citizen – Herself allowed him to do. I enjoyed the exercise but missed the longer, adventurous expeditions that we had once made. Rufus never shied again. Perhaps he was too old now, perhaps he had forgotten the vice, or perhaps, having been idle in the field for so long, he realised what had happened and had turned over a new leaf.

Then one day a terrible disaster and sadness hit us like a bolt from the blue. Herself was ill. She was coughing and spending the day in bed. In the past I had only understood about painful legs or backs, but now I understood that bad coughs were not comfortable things to have either, so I was sympathetic.

"My temperature keeps going up at night,", Herself said to Sandy. "So if I bring Rufus in in the morning, could you turn him out at night". Rufus was coming into the stable every day to avoid the flies and keep his figure trim and in the morning he came cheerfully trotting through the gate. Then Herself went back to bed. Just after I had had my dinner there was a terrible rumpus in the stable, the sound of Rufus' iron shoes scraping on the concrete floor. Herself leapt up and started to dress quickly. Then within seconds it stopped and she decided all was well and went back to bed. In the evening Sandy came to put Rufus out. He banged on the door. "There's something wrong with Rufus", he shouted up. "Will you come at once".

Rufus was standing rigid - his head right down and his eyes bright red. He looked stricken. Herself rushed indoors to telephone the vet, but the head vet was away and a young fellow came who we had never seen before. He had no idea what was wrong. "Look at the extraordinary cuts on his lips", Herself said to him, "and yet there is no blood. I'm sure he's dying. He was in great form in the morning. Someone must have done something dreadful to him in the stable and that was the noise I heard. Could those weird cuts be the way they forced his mouth open to put in some sort of poison? Oh why, why, did I not finish dressing and go out instead of thinking all was well when the noise stopped?".

Sandy tried to comfort her, "It would not have made any difference. If it was a gang they might have attacked you, and if they had gone you could not have done anything anyway. You cannot give an antidote if you do not know what is for."

"We would have gained time", Herself replied. "Now I'm sure it is too late. I seem to remember an incident here once before," she said turning to the young vet, "when Rufus' eyes were red like this and I thought someone could have thrown a substance into them", and she ran back into the house to see what had been recommended then. By the time she returned the young man had put white powder into Rufus' eyes which distressed her, because it seemed to make them worse.

"I think we should put him out into the air", said the vet. "It might give him a chance". It was a warm summer evening and he felt it would be easier for Rufus to breathe. But I could see Herself thought nothing could save him. Indeed it did not look as if they would be able to get him out, but they did, pushing, leading and encouraging. Although none of them were lacking in experience of horses no one knew what to do because no one knew what had happened. Later we went out three times - cough and flu' forgotten - and the third time Rufus seemed a little more cheerful and he ate a biscuit that we had taken out.

Then morning came. We went out very early and there was Rufus at the bottom of the field, rolled over on his back, with his feet and legs sticking up straight in the air. "Come away, Sherry", Herself said. I don't think she wanted me to see and we went back sadly into the house. Our friend was dead, and we will never know what happened to him. He had been so

[33]

gentle and friendly to me and I loved him and liked going for rides. Now all I have is a memory.

When Sandy arrived next day and Rufus had been taken away in a lorry, he reported that another pony had been killed in the same week. "It's in the newspaper", he said. "Someone with a shot gun shot the cover off an electric cable on a right of way, and, because the cable could not be seen in long grass, it electrocuted a pony ridden over it. The pony fell on its rider, who shouted to her friend, 'Don't touch me! You may be electrocuted also. Go and get help.' By the time help came the girl had managed to wriggle out from under the pony. It could have been an accident or it could have been done on purpose. Remember the dispute that is going on locally about horses and rights of way". "Very true", replied Herself. "The walkers are really angry about the horses making a mess of the woods and I've been told that vandals smashed the Community Association noticeboard simply because the secretary raised funds by running gymkhanas. There are 'anti's' about today who are not right in the head and will do anything to achieve their crazy aims."

Soon after that terrible sadness we moved house and went further north into a colder climate. I was not sorry to go because much of the happiness had gone out of my life. We could no longer go for rides and I no longer had my friend. Although there were no hardwoods further north, with tracks through them on which to walk or ride, and no bluebells except those we planted in the garden, there were fields and heather and brown hares and pheasants and moles and many interesting things to see and do.

CHAPTER VI

I Start my Training in Our New Home

Our new home in the north-east of Scotland, was square and creeper covered, with a wood on one side, a steading behind, and two fields running down to a burn. There was a high beech hedge to shelter the orchard and one of the fields, but the lawn and flower beds were windswept, protected only by a straggly rose hedge running along the road. Straightaway Herself planted more roses in the hedge and made a herbaceous border in front of it, which I could rootle through looking for rabbits. But there were no rabbits anywhere. They had all died of disease. What, therefore, could I do to be useful? I found there were moles living under the surface of the soil with underground passages, which ran on for hundreds of yards, giving off wonderful scents and usually leading to water. At intervals the moles surfaced and made mounds of earth through which I could dig to find their subterranean homes. There is no hope of a dog catching a mole because the passages are too small, but we can scare them off temporarily. Luckily they don't like coming up into flower beds, because the soft earth falls in on them. Whereas my scaring away of rabbits in the last garden had been popular, my attempt to scare the moles was quite the reverse, because it involved digging holes in the lawns and among the shrubs on the banks. So we hit on a compromise. I could dig in the orchard and the field and Herself dug in the flower beds and the bank.

To my great joy who should arrive for a week the next summer but my friend Sandy. We met him at the train and took him to stay at a farm. He came every day and dug and cut hedges and the next summer he came again. Sometimes also I went down to stay with him and his cat. But it was a long way for him to come and so the next summer Mr. Rennie came in his car to help, and we began to do all sorts of constructive things, like digging drains, laying patios and building walls. Mr. Rennie was tall and strong and had a little dog of his own, and he always noticed if I was not feeling well. He looked as if he would not stand any nonsense, but by this time I knew which part of the garden was mine and which was not, so we avoided trouble. Herself had bought a terrifying machine to mow the lawn on which she sat and over which she did not seem to have much control. Once she nearly went through a fence, so I kept well away, sometimes even going in doors, just in case it stole up on me unawares and ran me over.

I missed terribly not having a horse or pony to talk to and follow on rides, so when I was in London and saw horses of the same colour as Rufus in Hyde Park I tried to follow them. There was no hunting in this part of Scotland and instead of hearing the horn all we heard was the noise of gas guns scaring the birds off the crops. Because the farmers did not ride to hounds, they did not like horses on their land, thinking they cut up the grass and disturbed the stock. Also there were no big woods with wide tracks on which to ride, while out on the roads the lorries and cars, not understanding about horses, went very fast, making it very dangerous for a person to ride and a dog to follow behind. However, the farmer who was our nearest neighbour did allow us to walk through his fields, although they were full of sheep and cows. I knew about not disturbing stock, but sometimes I did so by mistake and Herself worried about my upseting him. Although there were no rabbits, there were brown hares and the moment I saw one I was gone in a flash, streaking off like a coursing Greyhound, everything that I had been taught forgotten in the chase. In one minute I was out of earshot and two fields away. She was told to use a stick that she could put quickly into the ground with a choker rope attached, which would run out as I ran. Suddenly the rope would tighten round my neck and I would be bowled over. I think Herself did not want to give me such a rude shock.

Then things took a surprising turn. We went out on a soaking wet day when the river was in flood. Suddenly I saw a hare and chased it, disappearing over a ridge and going like the devil. The hare went down to the river and disappeared from sight. I could not hear Herself shouting because of the wind and the ridge between us and anyway I'd no intention of stopping until the hare was caught or out of sight. I went along the river bank to see if it was hidden in the reeds. My head was down and my feet up and suddenly the soil gave way and I fell into the swollen river. I'd never been in water before and I was frightened, but instinct told me to paddle with my feet and luckily the current did not sweep me out into the middle but towards a little green promontory, where I could clamber out on to dry land. I was a very shaken and half drowned little dog. I could not hear Herself shouting, so I decided to go home and enter the garden by my secret route which officially I knew nothing about. When she arrived back some time later there I was by the door, soaked, terrified and shivering with cold. Was she pleased to see me? You can imagine just how pleased,

thinking I had been carried away in the swollen river. I never got into trouble for my disobedience, but I never ran away like that again. It was a much better lesson than a choker lead.

Lessons were becoming part of my life because I was by now nearly two years old. In the same way as I want to hunt out game and to retrieve it if it has been shot, I also wish to round up other animals and guard them. These two instincts are at odds with each other, and probably are one of the reasons why people say we are difficult to train. About this time I found a baby hare in the garden. I spotted it among the roses and I stood stock still until Herself came to see what was taking my attention. For a day and a half I was taken out on a lead in the hopes that if I did not scare it the mother hare would find it and take it home. But after a day and a half Herself decided she was not coming, so she picked the baby up and put it on a bed of grass in a cardboard box, feeding it 3 times a day with milk from a rubber filler. I stood in the kitchen all day, mesmerised by the hare, not sure whether it was a prey or a friend, but feeling that on balance it was my friend. It lived for a week and all that time I patiently guarded it and hoped it would be all right. But then it died, missing its mother's special milk. The farmer said we were silly to have interfered, "Baby hares can't take cow's milk. The mother would have come back in the end to find it". I wonder if he was right.

This event was an interlude in my training, which was not only to make me obedient, but also to prepare me for perhaps one day working as a gun dog. That is what Springers are bred for, to seek out and put up game for their owners to shoot and then to find and retrieve it. The birds are shot because they are good to eat and to prevent them suffering overcrowding and disease. We think they are good to eat too, so we have to learn to pick them up carefully and bring them straight back to our handler. We must not throw them down at the person's feet, which is impolite, or refuse to part with them, because the birds will be damaged. Herself threw an old woolly sock, filled with rags, for me to retrieve, which was soft so that it would not make my mouth hard when I carried it. I had to learn not to run after this dummy until I was given the order, and to mark carefully the line it was on and the distance away. Sometimes Herself hid the dummy in bushes or long grass without allowing me to watch. Then she would say "Hi! Lost!" and off I would go, sectioning the ground and going back and forth using nose and eyes to discover the hidden prize. We do this by instinct, but sometimes we go too fast or too far and have to be controlled by a whistle or a gesture, making us change direction or cover a piece of ground again.

I did not mind waiting for the order to retrieve, but I did not like sitting and staying on other occasions while Herself walked away, because, being over anxious, I thought she might never return. I once saw a man in Hyde Park, eating a sandwich as he walked away, who told his dog to wait until he was just a speck in the distance. Because the dog was a Labrador it did what it was told, but when it heard his whistle it had to run very fast to catch up with him again. I do try to sit still if I am told to, but even if I am in one part of a room and Herself is in another I will sneak across and sit upon her feet, just in case she tries to go, leaving me behind. Another thing I had to learn was to walk at heel and again , because they are camp dogs as well as retrievers, Labradors do this by instinct, whereas Springers like to walk a bit ahead to put up the game. "It's natural", said a gamekeeper, "for Springers to walk a yard or so in front. Don't worry. Just make sure she never goes further out than that, unless you tell her to". It was about this time that Sandy taught me to carry my own lead and this made me feel responsible for myself. So in the city I usually walked about 3 yards in front and waited for Herself at the end of the pavement, but in the country, if I was ranging free and there were other dogs about, I felt I had to rove further and further out to put up the game first and this was not at all popular with anyone.

When we were in London I often retrieved a tennis ball instead of a sock and perhaps this made me feel it was more a game than a job. We used to meet a Labrador in the gardens by the river, with his friendly owner, who threw sticks which the dog tirelessly retrieved. I enjoyed running after my ball, but one day, as I told you in an earlier chapter, my friend the Chelsea

Pensioner hit his hard little ball with his club and without being told to do so I retrieved it for him. Apparently this was not the right action to take, because he was playing golf and wished to hit the ball where it lay. When he said so in no uncertain terms I decided I had had enough of retrieving for the moment and that I would take a rest from the whole thing meantime. "Don't worry", said our friend, "she'll start again soon". But for a number of reasons I never did.

CHAPTER VII

Claustrophobia

During the winter months the most dreadful experience happened to me which I shall never forget. I was left for a whole fortnight by myself, without any human company that I knew, in a strange kennel, confined in a small space and surrounded by barking dogs. People say that most dogs are happy in kennels with other dogs all round them but I wasn't. I was terrified. Herself was going to a place she called 'abroad', which apparently is a place that dogs cannot go. We had gone from London to stay in the country with her relations. I had stayed there before and they were always kind to me. But on this occasion we set off in the car the day after our arrival to fetch their dogs from a kennel, where they had been staying for a few days.

I got a funny feeling - you know how you do - on the way over there that this was a trap and I was going to be left on my own. We arrived at this place and out of a wooden building bounced the two dogs - friends of mine - who were thrilled to see their owners and looked well and happy. All seemed well on the surface, but the feeling of doom that I had experienced in the car now came over me like a cloud. My collar was put on and I was led into a small confined place, with all around me the terrible noise of barking dogs. It was like a prison. No sooner had Herself gone than panic gripped me with power close to frenzy. Would she ever return? How was I to know how long I would be left? Would I be left there for ever? To make matters worse I had been too upset to listen to anything Herself had said about coming back and now I was hysterical with fear. I tore at the wooden bars of my kennel with my teeth, splintering the wood and yelling at the top of my voice.

Before long the kennel owners heard my cries and returned to see the damage I had done to their kennel. Not long after that Herself returned also. Hey presto! Was I pleased! It had worked! Overjoyed, I bounced back into the car. But alas, it was not to be! I had rejoiced too soon. 'Abroad' was somewhere I could not ever go and it was clear Herself was going - come what may. This was a situation I could never have imagined.   Within minutes we had arrived at another kennel where everything was made of concrete. I was left again with more strange dogs barking all round me. Herself disappeared down the passage and was gone. How could she have done that to me when she knew how frightened and upset I had been in the first kennel? How could she? Now I was angry as well as frightened and I tore at the concrete until my gums poured with blood and all the time I continued to yell at the top of my voice.

The kennel owners could not stop my panic, but they realised that I would kill myself if I went on like that. So they gave me little white pills to quieten me. These made me very sleepy and muddled in my mind, so that I staggered about and could not keep my balance. Before long I began to lose all sense of time and not to know whether it was morning or evening or how the days or nights were passing. After a bit I began to be very sick, whether from the pills, or the change of food or fright I do not know. I really began to wonder if I was going to come out of this experience alive and whether I would ever see my home again. I no longer had the energy or the will to howl or to tear at the concrete. I was too weak. By the time Herself returned two weeks later I was so dopey and sick that I could not even wag my tail in recognition. I was so changed that I felt she was wondering if I was the same dog. I had lost all sense of time and space. Naturally I was very relieved to see her as I am sure you can understand, but I was so hurt at being left in this manner for so long that I did not want to give her a welcome, even if I had not been feeling too sick and dopey to do so. We had to stop the car a number of times on the way back to London for me to be sick, and I kept myself to myself in the back of the car and did not engage in my usual conversation. It was not until I saw the passage to my own front door that I began to remember who I was and where we were and to know that I was home again.

We went to the vet at once and he gave me chocolates and medicine to stop me being sick. "In a case like this", he said, "the kennels have really no alternative but to give tranquilisers, but they have to give so many to take effect that it's not a good solution". At last by the end of the day the doping began to wear off and I decided to wag my tail and forgive and forget.

I was never left in a kennel again. When Herself went somewhere I could not go (either 'abroad' or to summer meetings when it was too hot in the car), I went to stay with Sandy and, after we moved north, with kind and friendly people on a farm who had a boarding kennel for dogs, which at first they tried to persuade me to live in. But I had heard them saying to Herself that they would take me into the house if necessary, so I just stood and wagged my tail and said with my eyes, "Please not", and they eventually allowed me to spend all my time with them in the house, where I joined a number of other dogs. They had sheep on the farm and Sheep-dogs and I soon chose what I would like to do. Every morning the husband went in the Landrover with Rover, the older Sheep-dog, to 'walk the sheep' (which means seeing that none were ill or stuck in a fence or had rolled over on their backs) and I asked if I could go too. When we returned to the farm I continued to sit in the Landrover for the rest of the day. Often Rover joined me, and so we became firm friends.

I enjoyed watching him working among the sheep, frequently driving them through a gate to move them from one field to another. Sheep naturally follow each other, but sometimes one breaks out from the flock, so that there is a right and wrong leader and a general muddle. Rover had to go very quickly and quietly to the spot where the wrong leader had bolted and lie down in front of the sheep to prevent them also breaking out. He might have to move a number of times before he had the sheep carefully herded in the right direction. Sometimes, even more difficult, it was necessary to take a single sheep out of the flock to check its feet or something like that. Rover would be shown the sheep and then by stalking and lying down he would corner it and keep it still, so that it could be caught with a shepherd's crook round its horn.

Very soon I had as much confidence in these kind people as I had in Herself and Sandy and I enjoyed sometimes going to stay there. Now I sit up as the car turns in off the road and I always check the boundaries for them on arrival to see if everything is still in order since my last visit. Once I was taken ill there in the night and they drove me over to my own vet in the morning, where I had an operation. By the time Herself came home I was quite better and chasing hares.

'Operation' was a word I came to understand all too well because I had four in all, of which this one was the third. They are not nice things to have, lumps and bumps are removed and you are stitched up again, but they make you feel better, so you have to put up with them. First of all you are sent to sleep with an injection, and then you know no more until you wake up wuzzy. The first time this happened I had got into a panic the moment I came round. Although I was staggering about and very sleepy I started screaming and breaking the place up. Herself had been told to telephone and when she did so they asked her to come back to London at once. When she arrived I staggered out to the car rolling from side to side and had to be helped in.

Next day the effect of the pain killers had worn off and I started tearing at the wound. By late evening I was very hot and Herself was frightened that I would re-open the wound. So off

we went to the emergency vets, who keep open all night. This was a interesting place, full of children with hampsters, cats and canaries, as well as dogs and puppies. After waiting our turn the lady vet clearly thought I was fussing. She was not sympathetic and gave me a large stiff collar, which I had to wear to stop me tearing at the wound. I could not see anything except just straight ahead. I could not even see my feet or how to get down the steps to the car. A young couple were passing on their way to a late night party and they stopped and spoke kindly to me amid bouts of almost uncontrollable laughter, which hurt my feelings.

"You look very funny", they said to me, "how on earth are you going to get into the car?" Between them and Herself I was manhandled in, but the cure was worse than the ill, so as soon as we were home Herself took off the horrid contraption, but she left it beside me and said that one more bite at the wound and she would put it on again.

Since then, as I have said, I have had three more operations and have learnt that, despite pain, discomfort and isolation, they make you feel better in the end, provided you lie quietly and wait for the wound to heal. In London and at home the vets who look after me have Springers of their own and understand how our minds work. We do get over-anxious and need reassurance, but at the same time we insist on our independence and do not like to be helped too much. I do not believe that, although she was always sympathetic, Herself really understood that dogs as well as people can suffer from claustrophobia. All this changed when one day we were both shut in the lift in our London home. It was the lift with the lattice doors and it suddenly stopped between floors. Although Herself was with me I was terrified. She regarded the whole thing as a joke and shouted and rang a bell. Louis the porter came to wind down the lift and release us. "So Sherry really does have claustrophobia", she said to him in a surprised voice. "I would not have believed it possible for a dog to suffer in that way". Clearly it was at this moment that she first realised how genuine my fears were.

CHAPTER VIII

I Become an Experienced Traveller

Normally, as I have explained, I go everywhere with Herself, so now I am really a very experienced traveller. My favourite form of travel is of course the car, although I do not like it if we drive too fast, in which case I go down on to the floor and do not look out. Otherwise I either sit up on the front seat and watch the traffic and scenery or I lie down and go to sleep. I know that when we put the flicker out - apart from the light it makes a funny noise - we are going to turn off the main road on to a side road and may be arriving at our destination. So, if I am snoozing, I wake up and take interest. Dogs recognise places, trees, roundabouts, turns in the road and all the other landmarks on roads just as people do, but in additon we have premonitions that we are about to arrive (and indeed that people are about to return) before the event actually happens. No one can explain how we do this and as we do not talk we are able to keep it a secret.

Unfortunately we cannot always go by car. Often in London Herself goes on her own on a bus and I am left sitting in the car, but occasionally I go in a bus with her. Sometimes we have to go upstairs where the atmosphere is smoky and the bus swings and lurches from side to side. Because the steps are steep and high it is very difficult to get down again on the lead and I nearly pull Herself off her feet. If someone else is getting off also then they take the lead and Herself goes first to prevent me getting off before the bus stops. When the bus is fairly empty or if the conductor likes dogs I am allowed to stay downstairs, but I have to tuck myself away under the seats. Just one or two

conductors like talking to dogs and then I am very happy being stroked and made a fuss of. Buses get us both to where we are going quicker than if we walk. Also I do not like going too far on pavements because they are hard on my feet and it takes quite a bit of concentration weaving one's way in and out of the crowds of people, carrying my lead. Once, on the way home from a shopping expedition (there is one shop in London which I am allowed into and where people always talk to me) I spotted a red bus stationary in a traffic queue, so, as I was ahead of Herself, I stepped off the pavement and boarded it. The conductor was cross, because he thought I was on my own and he would not know what to do with me. Herself rushed forward and took me off, apologising to the irate conductor. She said it was the wrong bus and would have taken us in the wrong direction, but as I did not realise this at the time, I sulked and walked as slowly as possible all the way home to show how tired I was and how my feet hurt and how I would have preferred a bus ride.

Then there are London taxis. I like them because there is lots of room to sit comfortably in the square compartment. Conversations between Herself and the driver go on all the time because the glass screen behind the driver is always open. The drivers like dogs. Many of them have dogs at home (which I can smell) and they like talking about them. If, when I am carrying my lead, a taxi stops beside me and people get out, then I try to get in to go for a ride, just as, when I was a puppy, I used to jump into the vans of tradesmen who came to work at the house. Once, not far from home, a tall, good-looking, well-dressed man got out of a taxi right beside me, so I went forward and, the door being open, started to jump in. He stepped forward at once to prevent me, but, being very polite, he gave a little bow and said, "I don't think I have the honour?". I stopped too and we stood and regarded each other in a friendly manner until Herself came up and apologised. She explained how, whenever I saw a taxi, I wanted to go for a ride. Not all strangers are so nice about my forwardness. One man was very annoyed when I tried to get into his taxi in the courtyard of the flats, so I have to be careful. But I know that the taxi drivers and many of the bus conductors in London are on my side. They are friendly people who like friendly dogs and are happy to have them in their cabs or buses.

The only terrifying form of travel is the train. I don't like this at all, but sometimes when we are going between Scotland and London in the winter I have to put up with it. If we are going from London then either we have to get on one bus with all our luggage and change to another or we have to get a taxi. When we arrive at the train station there are hundreds of people. It is like being on a crowded pavement, but much worse, because we are pulling a little cart with the luggage on it and I get all tied up in the lead. I cannot be allowed to carry my lead because, as with my reaction to the bangs and drums in the park, my fears are so strong that they would make me run away and go anywhere on earth rather than stay amid the terrible hubbub. Boarding the train is quite a business too. The step is so high I have to be helped in and once in motion the noise of the train worries me almost as much as the station. There is a horrible high-pitched whine which continues all the time and affects my ears, although, as I have grown older and gone a little deaf, it is not as bad as it once was. The noise increases to a crescendo when the train goes underground and the windows go dark, but it is there all the time. Apart from when we go through the tunnels I do not think people can hear it, but our Spaniel ears are very sensitive and it is truly painful. Even the thought of it makes me uneasy and on one occasion on the way to the train I got the shakes. I literally could not stop shaking and Herself was quite worried. We had arrived too early and had to queue, while a man kept announcing things on a loudspeaker which also hurt my ears.

Once on the train all I want to do is get out again, and if the door opened I would run away and end the nightmare. Isn't this silly? My fear would be worse if I was on my own. I know that the way to get out of the train is by the door at the end of the carriage. So I slip under the seat and start slowly working my way down under the seats towards the door, talking to any nice doggy pople that I find on the way. Sometimes Herself is working on papers and does not notice until I have gone quite a long way, but then she secures the lead round her ankles so that I cannot do it again. I am quite shrewd about knowing how long the journey takes and roughly whereabouts we are. On one occasion we were going to Berwick to stay with my friends Biddy and Jake, about whom I will tell you more in a later chapter. Berwick is a little more than half way home. I realised we were getting out soon because Herself got the luggage together and started moving down the train. I stood by the door waiting for the train to stop and the door to open. Once down on the platform I knew exactly where we were, although I had only been to Berwick station once before. So I took advantage of the moment that Herself was organising the luggage on to her cart and bolted for the stairs. I took no notice of her shouting my name above the general commotion. "Stop Sherry. Wait!" Not me. I wouldn't stop. I would get as far as I could in the shortest possible time from that noisy incarcerating prison. I remembered the lay-out of the station, so on my own I crossed the bridge in a crowd of people - I could hardly hear her voice now it was so far away - and dashed down the stairs on the far side, through the swing doors which someone opened for me and into the station yard.

I went straight to the parking place, where we had stopped on our last visit, checking each car to see which one my friends Biddy and Jake were in. They sit high up on a shelf at the back, so I can easily spot them from the ground. To my surprise and horror they were not there - so I really was all on my own - no car, no friends and now no owner, because Herself was a long long way behind, coming with the suitcases. Then I suddenly spotted the white car that I knew belonged to our friends turning into the station yard and drawing up to park in a line of other cars. Off I went at great speed wagging my tail and saying, "Stop. Please. I want to get in". Perhaps I was lucky not to have got run over because traffic was moving all round me, but I thought it was pretty clever to know my way round the station and yard when I had only been there once before and so

did every one else, so I was not ticked off. As I explained earlier, dogs are like that. They remember places very clearly, particularly places where they have been happy.

I have one travel story, however, about which I am ashamed. We were driving south and were going to stay for a night with Biddy and Jake. When almost there we rounded a corner and saw an expanse of water on the road and a car coming the other way. So we went into the water. The next day we went into the nearby town before leaving for London, but when Herself returned to the car it would not start. Consternation followed. A garage man arrived and so did Biddy and Jake in their car with Mrs. L. 'Hooray', I said to myself because the man made the car go at once. He left, but we only went a few hundred yards and it stopped again. There was more telephoning. Mrs. L arrived again and they went to have lunch. Then a man in uniform arrived in a car with signs on it. Eventually he made the car go and we went back to the house, but next day the car had hiccups, so there was more worry. We went to fill up with petrol and the garage owner came out and said kindly that he would help. He got into the car and switched on the engine. I am always safe when mechanics get into the car. I do not guard it because I know that these men are like vets and put things right. But in this town it seemed no mechanic could cure our car. So I decided to guard it and I flew over the front seat and took him by the arm with my teeth. Luckily he had on a padded jacket and I realised at once my mistake, so no harm was done and I was very apologetic. Fortunately he was not cross and he was reassuring about the car. He said, "The trouble has been caused by the water. The car will get you to London, but keep it running all the time". Once Herself had loaded the car we didn't switch the engine off until we reached London and stopped at the Park to see the squirrels.

CHAPTER IX

I Am Found to be Gun Shy

Do you remember I told you how I suddenly refused to retrieve and that we were advised I would soon regain my interest. Before this happened, however, I became 'gun shy', which put an end to my training as a retriever. I could not stand any more loud noises. No one knew the cause, but everyone had a theory. "Perhaps", someone said to Herself, "it's because you shot rabbits from the top floor windows of the last house. There's greater reverberation of sound within a building". Another person suggested, "Didn't you say Sherry got a fright when there was a bomb in Knightsbridge, that would put her off loud bangs?", and a third said, "Wasn't there was a story of jets flying low overhead when she was tiny? Perhaps the wailing sirens in London - police, ambulance, car and house alarms remind her of that". Certainly I did not like these city noises, but then neither did I like the gas gun going off at home to frighten the birds away from the crops. I always went indoors whenever I heard it. Now, even when noises of shooting and banging came from the side of the sitting room where stood the box on legs I went to another room. "It's only the television", Herself would say clearly, hoping I would recognise the word and realise the box was harmless, but that did not stop me leaving. I no longer liked noises of any kind. They hurt my ears. The truth now had to be faced. If I was gun shy it was not worth carrying on with my training and Herself decided to refuse any suggestion that I should pick up birds after shoots.

The moment my training stopped I became wayward again. I had always shown a desire to range too far out when I was with other dogs. Now this urge became stronger and if there were lots of rabbits, as there were in the mountains, where Herself's cousins lived, the temptation was over-powering. We went there often on a day's visit and I enjoyed the scents of rabbits, grouse and blue hares (which are grey in summer, but turn white in the winter so that you cannot see them in the snow). One day I was walking with Herself and her cousins and their two Labradors, Karen and Poppy. They were ranging within sight and hearing. but, in order to be sure I found the game first, I was ranging further and further out. I knew that I should not be doing this and Herself kept running in front of the others, whistling and calling to try and control me. On the way home, just to show off to the Labradors, whom I secretly regard as being a bit goodie goodie - they work on the hill in the grouse shooting season, so they have to be well-behaved - I disappeared into a thicket, where there were rabbit holes, and refused to come out, regardless of shouts and whistles. I could hear a discussion going on about my behaviour and whether or not I would have to be beaten for my disobedience. "I don't know what to do", Herself was saying, "I'm at the end of my tether. She's getting worse and worse. Either I'll have to beat her or she'll have to go". It sounded the sort of conversation, judging by the tone of voice, that I had heard when Sandy's intervention had saved me. Now I was hauled out by the scruff of my neck and disciplined. Was it that that brought me to my senses, or the tone of Herself's voice when she said, "I'm at the end of my tether. She will have to go"? Or was it for another reason altogether that I improved? On the way back we met Geordie, the keeper, who looks after the grouse on the hill, burning the old heather that they don't eat and – always keeping within the law – controlling the dangerous predators, which kill them and eat their eggs. He let Herself into a secret about how to make dogs obey the whistle. "If they won't come back", he said, "blow the the whistle very loud right up close to their ears. Whenever they hear it afterwards they will come back at once. They can't stand the thought of the pain it gives them". That worked and my behaviour on hill walks began to improve.

People forget that dogs from working strains require a job, just like people do. They must be occupied. Now I was being bossed about by people who no longer wanted to employ me because I was frightened of noise. Nor, it would appear, did they want me to be self-employed, putting up and running after game myself, particularly when I was walking on other people's land. What, therefore, could I do to occupy myself? I had a brain wave. If Herself wanted to boss me about, then I would boss her about in return. Her job had to do with writing things on paper and sitting in front of a screen (a silent screen this time), using her fingers to hit keys. Her routine was to get out of bed at six and go down to have breakfast, after which she came back to bed to write for two or three hours before getting up. I made a point now of getting up at six also, telling her to get up if she was not up already and then going back to bed myself. If, when she came back to bed, she did not start to write at once I went and sat beside her to remind her to begin her

work. People ask how it is that dogs know the time. This is another secret we have. We do not need to look at clocks. We just know the time by instinct. Likewise, if she was sitting by the fire downstairs doing nothing I would go across and ask her why she was not reading or writing and, if she was not busy, I suggested that perhaps she would like to talk to me. Meanwhile I kept my side of the bargain and remained in touch when we were out on the hill or in the fields.

When I was walking with Poppy and Karen they told me about their work on the hill and why it is that shooting dogs have to be so disciplined. On the 12th of August and for two weeks afterwards the grouse are shot by a method known as 'walking up'. The dogs walk at heel through the heather beside their owners and guests, while the keepers, with game bags slung over their backs, also have their Labradors walking beside them. They fan out over the hill and it is important that they keep in a straight line to avoid people shooting each other. When they change direction the people and dogs on the outside of the wheel have to go faster than those on the inside. When a single bird or a covey of birds gets up out of the heather in front of the guns and some are shot the line temporarily stops and the dogs are sent out to retrieve the fallen birds. The people and dogs walk many miles each day up and down the mountains until the whole moor is covered in this way. Once upon a time a pony with panniers followed behind the line, but now it is a tiny tractor or 'argo cat' which takes the game at intervals from the keepers' bags. Sometimes special dogs called Pointers are employed to walk in front of the line of guns, and these dogs stop when they scent a grouse, one paw raised. This gives people more time to pick out and shoot the old birds in a covey. The young grouse are much more succulent to eat, as I know from the left-overs on the plates, but it protects the species and the moor to shoot the old birds and leave the young for next year.

After the fortnight is past then the driving season begins. People with flags go far out over the mountains and then line out and walk back towards a line of butts (or dug-outs), where the guns and their loaders are hidden. The grouse fly at great speed over these butts and it is only the expert shots who can bring a grouse down, so many escape. The dogs stay with their owners or with their keepers, who may be in the butts or positioned out on the flanks, and when the drive is over the dogs pick up the fallen birds, which they have seen fall and marked in their memory or which they find and retrieve entirely by scent.

Once on the cousins' moor I went to a gun dog trial, in which dogs compete to see which is the best retriever. I was taken out on a lead and walked with the spectators behind the line of guns, dogs and handlers. The dogs can be helped by their trainers with whistles and hand signals to pick up the grouse shot by the guns. Sometimes a number of dogs compete at the same time, because if the first dog fails to find the bird a second dog is sent out and so on. The line of guns and dog handlers moves forward together and when a grouse gets up and is shot, the dog whose turn it is goes forward to find and retrieve it. First it quarters the ground, going back and forth across each section. Sometimes it loses marks by 'running in' - going off too soon after it hears the shot, sometimes it quarters the ground too fast because it is too keen and pays insufficient attention to the scent. These dogs have to be summoned back by their trainer's whistle and lose marks. If a bird is wounded and becomes a 'runner' it must be retrieved to save it from dying a painful death. I knew one of the dogs, a little black Labrador called Nick, a neighbour of ours, who was younger than the others. When her turn came she marked the grouse, but another dog ran in and stole it, so when the line moved forward again she walked 3 feet ahead of her owner in case she lost another bird the same way. Realising she was anxious the judge let her do this, although she should have been at heel. The next bird shot fell at the back of a peat hag. Off went Nick too far to the left. Her owner whistled, 'Stop'. She obeyed and, following her owner's signal to the right, she found and picked up the grouse, giving her top marks. Immediately another grouse rose, but hearing her owner's whistle, she continued back with her bird. She only paused for a minute, but the judge counted the pause as a 'run in' and asked for her to be put on the lead. Down by the river another chance came. A snipe had fallen and was a runner and the first dog failed to find it. Nick's legs being short she had to run down the line of fence to cross it and then to come back to where the snipe had fallen. When she got there it flew away, so she returned. "That's not the same bird", said the judge and went to investigate. But Nick was right, the bird had gone. When the prizes were given out in the barn the winner was a Springer Spaniel, so, although I would have liked Nick to win a place, I was very proud of my breed.

CHAPTER X

A New Pony

While these activities were going on, we still had no horse or pony for Herself to ride and me to follow. Indeed, what would we have done with one, for, although we could walk on our kind neighbour's fields, we could not ride. What we needed was a right of way - a bridle path - and many times we went down to the old railway line, with Herself hoping that, if we could get access to it, we could ride along the track - although I found the wooden sleepers rather slippery. So hopeful was she of success that in the summer we even went to try out three horses with a view to buying one, but luckily there was something wrong with each of them, for the next thing we heard was the 'chug chug' of an engine on the newly opened tourist line. This was the first holiday excursion train and Herself knew that we had no hope of getting our bridle path now.

So what could be done with the grass in the fields and no animal to eat it? The solution was to make hay, but it was mixed with so much weed it could only be given away to the farmer who cut it with a tractor. I enjoyed this because it meant hours of work turning the hay and collecting it into 'huicks', during which time I could excavate. But it was hard work with no reward, so a friendly flock of sheep came as tenants. But a few had mild foot rot, which made them lame - very common in sheep, whose feet have often to be inspected. Almost at once I started getting itchy places on my back legs, which I scratched and bit with my teeth until they bled. Although the vet gave me pills and shampoo the trouble persisted and when we went to London I was given a purple spray and lacing boots with the feet cut out to stop me scratching. Whoever heard of a Springer Spaniel in boots? Still, however, the trouble persisted - for months and then a year - so that I was driving myself and everyone one else crazy. At last concerned friends recommended an animal skin specialist, who gave us different pills and another shampoo and ointment and said the trouble was caused by bacteria in the clay soil. "Yes", he said, "it might be related to foot rot in sheep". So the sheep did not come back in the summer and when the itch still persisted, Herself said one day in desperation, "We'll do all three cures at once - pills, shampoo, spray, ointment, boots - altogether". So we devoted almost two hours a day to the task, one in the morning and one in the evening and at last, hey presto, I was cured!

This meant we had to go back to making hay, and Mr. Rennie, now older, had to slide down off the high-loaded trailer, so Herself worried about him as well as being troubled about all that work with no reward. So the following summer the part-time shepherd offered her a cow and calf instead of the sheep. After a week or two, when they had eaten the grass in one field, Mr. Rennie said, 'I think the cow is lame'. Just then my legs became scratchy again and I began tearing at them with my teeth and making them sore. After taking advice and looking up books Herself replied to Mr. Rennie, "Apparently it could be 'foul of the foot', which is the cattle equivalent of foot rot in sheep. Instead of moving them to the next field, perhaps we should ask for them to be taken away". Next day the trailer arrived into which the calf walked straight away, but the cow did not wish to leave and took off at a hand gallop. It jumped the fence and leapt into the river, wading up its bed until it could climb out on the other side. Herself started running, but then fetched the car and off we went on an exciting chase after the disappearing cow, which suddenly reappeared – after jumping eight gates – amongst the bullocks, which daily regarded me with curiosity from the other side of our road. Once the cow had gone my legs stopped itching, but this time Herself could not face making hay, so the grass got higher and higher and when I was looking for moles I could not see where I was going amid the jungly stalks. It looked so untidy that, when we met our friend the shepherd on the road, Herself said, "Perhaps you should send the cow back after all. There can't be much wrong with its feet if it jumped 8 gates". Politely he replied with a smile, "I think on balance it might be too much trouble". So the next summer Herself decided to buy a 3-year-old Shetland pony, which could eat the grass and be broken in to harness in order to pull a cart and save Mr. Rennie from pushing the wheelbarrow. Off we went to a horse sale, where there were cars, landrovers, trailers, lorries, horses and ponies. When we got home Jo arrived in a lorry all by himself. He was very good looking, a bright red chestnut, with thick mane and tail. He seemed to like dogs, but he was a bit bouncy and had to be told not to chase me around the field.

When I got to know him better I found that, unlike Rufus, Jo was a funny little chap, with lots of quirks. When he first came he was terrified of sticks and of anything that looked like a stick (such as a stable broom) and he did not like sudden noises or movements. He was frightened of men and it took him 2 years to even take a carrot from Mr. Rennie, who was always kind. Nevertheless he did not do what people wanted him to do, but was determined to get his own way. He enjoyed fighting people and getting worked up into a rage. Herself talked to him a lot, explaining and reassuring, and he did listen, and when he got angry she stood and laughed, which made him calm down. If he refused to go through a gate she ran out a length of rope and drove him from behind. Eventually he realised that he must do what he was told, but it took a long time to explain this to him. While Mr. Rennie was making a wooden cart with rubber wheels, Herself had to tame Jo sufficiently to break him in to harness and encourage him to go safely between the shafts. While I was looking for moles in the field she put Jo on a lunging rope, making him walk, trot and canter in a circle. At first, he charged off in all directions and she was towed after him, but only once did she let go. Soon he got the idea and enjoyed the exercise. If he was doing well and being told he was a good pony I got jealous and crossed in front of him to put him off his stride, but if he was doing badly then I comforted him instead. Then a riding saddle was put on and Herself drove him about in long reins, stopping and starting as if he was being ridden. Jo enjoyed all this and so did she, so when an expert lady brought an experienced child to ride him Jo behaved very well until a motor bicycle passed on the road, and he nearly jumped out of his skin, causing the child to be quickly removed from his back. In fact the riding was so successful that Jo went off for two weeks schooling in an indoor school. By this time he regarded us as his adopted family so he screamed and neighed all the way up the road in the lorry, "Please don't send me away". However he must have enjoyed himself when he got there because he came home much improved.

That turned out to be easy, however, compared with putting him in the cart. The grandchildren, who were staying at the time, pushed the cart all round him to get him used to it. Herself knew nothing about driving ponies, so, although Mr. Rennie had driven young cart horses, off we went to a demonstration, where she was told that the pony must first tow a rubber tyre or wooden bar. Jo was frightened of the tyre, but he did not mind the bar, which was attached to his breastplate with long ropes on either side of the bar. Everything was all right when Mr. Rennie was there, they never took a risk and it was easier with two people. But one day Herself was on her own. Unexpectedly Jo panicked. He did this sometimes. Just in a minute he would go mad for no apparent reason. Then a rope broke with him still attached to the other one. Round and round he went on the single rope, with it getting tied round his legs. Herself hung on to him, goodness knows how, but she could not get close enough to unclip the rope. Eventually the staple came out of the wood, and he was free. There he stood, terrified, with his flanks heaving, looking so dejected that I went up to him and did what Rufus had done to me as a puppy, I put my nose right

up against his nostrils and blew into them saying, "Don't take any notice of these human beings. They really do the most stupid things"

But Shetlands are funny ponies. They are naughty for naughtiness' sake and that lands them in difficulties. Just as things were going better a caper of Jo's nearly landed him in disaster. By this time Herself and Mr. Rennie had joined the towing ropes to an old bit of carpet. The cart still required finishing touches and Herself had thought it would give Jo the idea of pulling something a little heavier before harnessing him to the cart, which he could destroy if he went wild through fright or wickedness. Jo rather liked his bit of carpet and was towing some quite heavy loads. We were walking towards the field. Herself was at his head and she turned round to speak to Mr. Rennie, who was at the back. Jo suddenly had a bright thought. Tucking his head down with his right ear forward he slipped his bridle off, a very difficult thing to do without the aid of a post, but apparently, so Herself was told afterwards, a favourite Shetland trick. The next second Jo was careering round the high lawn on his own with the carpet behind him. It looked funny, but if he had jumped off the rocky bank, which is five feet up from the drive, it would not have been funny at all. Then he galloped back down the path, ducked his head and shot through a line of trees and a wire fence into the field, knocking out just one staple, which gave him room between the wires – the carpet still attached. It was an extraordinarily agile thing to do and nothing was broken. But it gave him a bad fright and he might have been seriously injured.

This time I did not comfort Jo. I thought he had been silly. The incident set back his progress and it was not until next summer that they got him safely into the cart. At the start, while they hitched him up and buckled him in, Herself kept talking to him and feeding him with carrots, which diverted his attention. Then she and Mr. Rennie took a rein each and led him between them. Jo was so good that sometimes I was jealous and crossed in front of him to put him off his stride.

Mr. Rennie and Herself took it in turns to walk at his head, while the other one took the long reins at the back. That continued until Herself could drive him from the back of the cart with no one at his head. Was I brave enough to take a ride? Luckily so far no one has asked me.

CHAPTER XI

My Friends

As you can see from my story dogs have friends, just like people do. Some of my friends are people, some are dogs, others are ponies or cats. I also, if you remember, had a friend in London who was a white rabbit, although what would have happened if the wire had not been there to separate us I am not sure. We know at once whether people like us or not. If they do then we make friends, if they do not then we leave them alone. We are good at keeping in with those on whom we depend and this is called making 'cupboard love', because it depends on what is on offer in the cupboard. After we had moved house and went back to see Sandy it was sometimes difficult to know whether I was going to be left there or not. So I would go and sit beside Herself, hoping I could be taken with her, then I would move over to Sandy to tell him how much I liked him, in case I was to be left there - and I would go back and forth until the visit ended and I was told whether I was staying or going. The main way that we show people we like them is by sitting beside them and lying by their feet.

In London I made acquaintances among the dogs in the parks and no enemies. This is, as I have told you, because the park is neutral ground so no one starts a fight and dogs approach one another wagging their tails. But things can be different if you go to people's houses and gardens, particularly if the dog is of the same sex. One of my favourite places to stay on our way home is near a big river, upstream from where Biddy and Jake live. I know when we turn off the main road at the bottom of the hill where we are going. A long wide tarmac farm road, lined with tall trees on either side, leads to the house and farm. The people are welcoming and there are lots and lots of pheasants. You can imagine how happy that makes me, but I have to be careful not to disturb them, particularly when they are nesting. Either I have to be put on the lead or answer every call to come to heel.

There is a Bedfordshire terrier there, whose name is Winnie, and we were once firm friends. She always welcomed me and never told by any of the usual signs that she resented me. We lay on the floor together and she showed me her favourite places when we walked. Then one day we were going down a garden path running near the fence, which bounds a favourite field for pheasants. Perhaps I said something about the pheasants, which after all are on her property. Suddenly with no warning she flew at me and sank her teeth into the fur of my neck, which is fortunately quite thick. Herself and Mary, to whom the house belongs, shouted at us and one of them suggested getting water, but we were a long way from the house, so they got hold of us by our backsides and pulled and shouted our names. Lo and behold it worked! Winnie suddenly let go the tremendous hold she had on my neck and became quite friendly again. We have never been allowed to meet again, which is sad. When we go to stay either I sit in the car or Winnie is shut in the kitchen. I wonder if she is as sad about it as I am.

I've told you already about Jake, the miniature Dachshund, and Biddy, the Border Terrier. I know exactly where their house is and as we turn the car across the road I become so excited that I try to get out before the door opens. Biddy came to replace Tatters, who died of a disease the vets could not cure. Tatters was a mongrel and she inherited little bits of everything terrier - hence her name. She was small and wiry and very naughty. She led Jake an awful dance. He adored her and together he followed her down every precipice to the river and explored every hole on its banks. There is a third house, which we also visit in the same countryside - tall and white, surrounded by trees and fields, with the three Eildon hills rising behind. There are lots of dogs there, Benji, an Alsatian, two Labradors and two Norwich Terriers. I am frightened of Benjie and so is Herself, despite knowing him as a puppy. If we arrive to stay and either we are early or the family are late, Herself will not get out of the car but looks at Benjie through glass. Stories are told about little pieces he has - or has not - taken out of people calling unannounced at the house. He has to be master - top dog - of every situation.

Everything you could want to see and do surrounds you on walks from this house - there are cattle, sheep, hares, rabbits, pheasants, pigeons, burns running with clear water, mud, undergrowth, gorse bushes and fallen trees with hollow trunks. Benjie gives orders as we start out and every dog has to obey. Every dog that is except Tatters when she was alive. She was frightened of nobody and nothing. She came from a long line of hunt terriers, employed to force foxes out of their lairs. She never boasted about it, but if your ancestors can fight foxes and win you would not want to be bossed about by an Alsatian. These walks are a paradise for dogs and for Tatters and Jake the underground network of holes was a temptation. Mrs. L often kept one of them on the lead as a hostage for most of the walk – and then just as we were getting back to her sister-in-law's house she would relent and give them both a free run. That was enough. Off they would go at full gallop and Tatters would lead Jake to a hole she had spotted. Everyone would worry for hours about whether they were stuck down it. Little dogs burrow on and on in these underground caverns and then, when they want to back out again, their fur is lying the wrong way and there is not sufficient push in their legs to reverse. There they are, stuck, until starvation makes their tummies smaller and they can, if they are lucky, wriggle out days later.

Sometimes dogs fail to find their way back to the surface. The two little Norwich Terriers also loved hunting, although they were not as naughty as Tatters. They were gone once for five days and even then the mother did not return, only the daughter. No one knows what happened to the mother and that left a sadness, as when Tatters died. Jake had been inconsolable then. I tried to cheer him up when we went there but it had little effect. He stayed in his basket all day and even when Biddy came he did not cheer up at once. However, because she never left him alone for a second she eventually brought him back to life.

When we are in London we often go to the country for the week-ends, where some friends have dogs and some do not. All the places that we go to give me a big welcome so I like visiting. The grandchildren have a Golden Retriever called Elsa, who occasionally goes shooting, but she is so gentle and well mannered that she prefers life at home. A longer drive brings us to Hester and Mollie, who are black Labradors. They greet you like their owners do, as if you had never been away. So I feel at home at once and go off down the garden to see if everything is still in order, including the fish in the pond. There is very little game there, so we walk very happily together, not having to take matters seriously. Further on again we stay with friends who have a lake, the banks of which are wonderful to explore. At one time they had a Gordon Setter, who was huge but very gentle and a good companion. Now they have a Deerhound, who is so big he knocks you flying by mistake and I have to ask to be put back on the lead or into the car.

Sometimes in London or at home I am asked into the house when Herself goes out to lunch or dinner. When we set out in the car hope springs eternal, but I am only asked in about half the time. When Herself starts getting clothes out of the cupboard I check on them to see whether this will be a small party, which I can probably attend, or a big party, which I cannot attend. The smarter the clothes the less likely that I shall be asked in. I only show my disappointment when we draw up to a house where usually I am welcome and this time I am left in the car. On these occasions I sulk when Herself returns and I turn my back on her and look out of the window. It is a good idea, if it is a house where I am usually welcome, to whine as she gets out to remind her that she should ask permission to bring me. But sometimes I realise it is hopeless. There are too many people coming for them to want a dog.

I also like people coming to our house. I know they are coming because there is extra activity in the kitchen. Then if we are at home, Herself will go out and get flowers and when she starts to lay the table in the dining room I know that we are definitely having visitors. At that point I go to the carved wooden box under the window that looks out on the front gate to check who is going to be driving their car up to the front door. In the country people do not make such a fuss of dogs as they do in London, because most people have dogs of their own, but sometimes they bring dogs with them and that is good because then I can play host back again. Karen and Poppy come with the cousins and they are as well behaved in our house as they are on the moor. Jake and Biddy come to stay and try to go under the wire fence in order to go hunting. Another friend in Scotland is Ceeki who is a Corgi – it was in her garden that we were attacked by a ferret. People say Corgis are uncertain tempered, but Ceeki is not. We did fight once but that was because someone dropped food during a party in our house and we both claimed it. She said her people had dropped it, and I said it was my house. But we stopped fighting the moment we were told to stop.

Now I am going to finish this chapter by telling you about my special friends in London who do not have a dog now but always had a dog before. They keep a ball for me in the drawer of the writing desk. I know when we turn at the traffic lights many streets away that we are going to their house and I sit up very straight and take notice, ready to jump out of the car the moment it comes to a halt. When the door opens I am waiting behind it and in I bolt, straight across to the writing desk to get my ball. Their names are Pam and

Tom. I know I am a very important person to them and they are very important people to me, I will tell you how important in the next chapter.

CHAPTER XII

I Am Very Ill

When we were in London in the winter I was always happy staying with Pam and Tom if Herself was in Scotland for a day or two. It meant I did not have to go on that dreadful train. Their little house is close to Hyde Park, so we could walk there and if it was a weekend we could go to the golf course, where Tom played golf, and walk off the course among the whin bushes. If during the week he took his clubs and played golf, I would sit in the car until he fetched me and then we would both walk alongside the course, where there were lots of scents and wonderful views. Then Tom became ill and walked with two sticks and when we returned to London he was not there any more and Pam was sad, and on her own. So when we went to her house I sat beside her to sympathise that half her life had come to an end. She was always pleased to see us, which was fortunate because we were suddenly hit by disaster.

That year when we returned to London, everything in the flat seemed normal. Then Herself noticed small golden bodies in my basket and when she turned the basket over she saw they had bored into the wicker. We showed them to the porters who said they were tiny moths. A day or two later she noticed a mark on a rug like a stain and when she turned the rug over the wool was eaten down to the backing. Then she found other rugs in the same state. Underneath all of them was black sticky stuff which had apparently come from a black travelling rug in a drawer - thick enough to be a carpet - which the moths had devoured, and then trailed the residue all round the flat. She was very worried and we went to the shop, which I was allowed to visit, and bought wool. All day and every day she sat mending rugs. Then she started to telephone.

"I don't believe it", she said to the person at the other end of the line. "You say these tiny golden moths are a special type of house moth which only eats carpet wool. And you say that they are carried by pigeons which breed in their nests. It's like something

out of the Arabian nights". But the vermin specialist to whom she was talking was right, for a pigeon's nest was discovered the next day on a balcony above our sitting room window and the moths had apparently flown in from there or from the back of a pigeon passing our window on the way to the nest.

"I can see what's happened", she said to the head porter. "Every time my son came into the flat for a night while we were away, he opened the windows and in came the moths. Then every time he left he shut the windows and the moths were trapped inside. What is amazing is the speed at which they eat and breed. Everything seemed fine when I was here only two months ago. Now the vermin man says we must have the flat sprayed with chemicals to kill the moths, for otherwise we'll never get rid of them. I've taken the cheapest quote. I wonder if it was wise".

A week later two men dressed in boiler suits and carrying containers and masks came to spray the flat. They told Herself she must leave the flat for at least six hours afterwards and she arranged with friends to be away for a night. Christmas was coming in three days time and most people, including Pam, were leaving or had left London. "Don't worry", said friends, who were staying in London. "Come to us. There's a clause in the lease to say No Dogs, but it won't matter for one night". So Herself packed a case and when the men had finished off we went. I sat in the car, which was parked beside the street in front of the block of flats, while the three of them, Herself and her friends went off to a restaurant. When they got back they opened the car door and discussed taking me into the building, but on second thoughts they decided to leave it until bed-time. When bed-time came they returned worried and disturbed. The husband said he had lost his nerve because he was applying for a new lease and might not get it if the landlords heard he had had a dog for a night. "Couldn't you leave Sherry in the car?", he asked. "Not in London", Herself replied, and used her mobile telephone to ring a young cousin, who had just moved house over the river. "Yes", he said, "You can come here, but you'll have to bring bed and bedding". So off we went to collect these from the flat and find the cousin's new home in the dark. Suddenly in the middle of the night Herself woke with a racking cough. She could hardly get breath. "Damn", she said, "this pillow came from a cupboard which must have been sprayed with chemicals". There was no furniture yet in the bedroom and nothing to use as a pillow, so she wrapped her clothes into a bundle and put her head on that. In the morning she was no better and visited the doctor, who gave her a prescription for pills, which we picked up from our friend the chemist. "The doctor says I have sheep dip syndrome", she told him. "Apparently the stuff they use for these sprays is the same as the chemical they use for sheep dip".

Together we returned to the flat and found the smell had gone. For a week Herself was ill in bed with a cough and missed Christmas. A kind friend who lived in a flat in the same building came and took me for walks and brought us food. I enjoyed our walks together. As soon as Herself was better we went down to stay with the family and it seemed everything was returning to normal. But it was not. When we got back to London we found the moths still flying round the flat. There seemed more now than before. Herself killed them between the palms of her hands in mid air, making a horrid clap, which frightened me. The head of the firm came to see us and said he was sorry she had been ill and, because his firm should not have sprayed the pillows, he would credit her with the doctor's fee. He told us that the flat must be sprayed again. "No", said Herself. "Not again. The cure is worse than the disease". But the doctor took a different line. "Of course you must get it done again, you cannot share your home with carpet moths. But you must be out of the flat for a week because you will now be allergic to the chemicals".

Pam was happy for us to stay with her for as long as we wanted, so Herself agreed to have the job done and in consultation with the head porter she decided to leave the windows shut for five days to make sure the moths were dead. On the sixth day we went back to open them. The smell was appalling, so she sat reading her post and writing letters at the entrance of the flat, where there was air coming in from the passage window. I decided to be independent and go to the dining room, where the smell was not as bad, and to sit under the tallboy where the carpet did not smell at all. After half an hour we returned to Pam's house leaving the windows open until nightfall. On the afternoon of the fourth day, when we were shutting the windows for the night, Pam came for tea on her way home from work. As I got up from my basket to leave the flat my legs suddenly spreadeagled and I fell down. My head was muzzy, my limbs were floppy and I was unable to walk. Somehow Herself and Pam got me to the car where I was terribly sick. Then half carrying me they took me to the gardens where I was sick again. But my legs would not carry me and now my eyes had gone into a terrifying judder, so that I could not see because the outside objects were moving quickly this way and that. I was panic- stricken.

We went to the Emergency Vets where I collapsed on the floor. Herself sat beside me stroking me to give me confidence. A young man examined me and said I was suffering from inflammation of the arteries of the brain. "I'm 75% certain it is caused by the chemicals in the spray, but it is a condition that some older dogs can produce." He said I must have two lots of pills and that he would like to keep me over-night. "No", said Herself, "she will panic and fret. We will nurse her". "Don't worry too much", he volunteered, "it is a condition from which dogs can recover. Come back tomorrow". Pam and Herself nursed me devotedly in her house. They helped me up from my basket, helped me out to spend a penny, helped me up and down stairs and gave me pills a number of times a day. Soon my eyes began to improve and I could see things steadily again. Then after a bit my legs strengthened. I never realised before how much I was loved and that gave me security and hope and made me determined to respond and get better. When we returned to the vet he was amazed at the extent of my recovery.

After a week we went to the country to stay with cousins and friends and I enjoyed the fresh air. But when we went back to the flat, although we had broken our routine and left the windows open by night as well as by day the smell was no better, so we stayed in Pam's house and Herself shampooed the carpets twice. Even when we did return - "You're making this decision, not me", Pam said hospitably as we drove off – for a whole week we still had to open every window in the flat in the evening and (because it was still mid winter) go elsewhere for an hour or two, until the rooms had aired sufficiently for us to sleep safely.

I felt older and a bit battered and so I could see did Herself, but the moths were dead and the earth and pigeon's nest were removed, and wire netting was erected to prevent the birds returning. This time Herself felt the sprayers had made no mistakes – the head man had come himself to supervise – but they both thought there was something wrong with the chemical . "Oh no", said the international firm that made it, "there's nothing wrong with our chemicals. They are odourless and harmless". They repeated this so often and so vehemently that, as Herself told her friends, it seemed unlikely she was ever going to convince them otherwise. "Black becomes white", she said, "when distance divides."

All that coming summer we spent as much time as we could in the fresh air, whatever the weather. "That was what I found after the effects of sheep dip", a farming friend advised Herself, "I don't know why, but I always felt better in the fresh air during or after dipping. That seemed to all of us to bring the most improvement and counter the effects of the chemicals." We heeded his advice and slowly began to regain our energy and to wake from what had been a nightmare.

CHAPTER XIII

Water, Water Everywhere

Although undoubtedly I made a good recovery I was never quite the same after this alarming experience, but perhaps it was also that the years were beginning to take their toll. In fact I will have to end my story soon because I am getting forgetful and rather breathless. From time to time I fall over sideways, although I am up and on before I hope anyone has noticed. Also ever since my illness I need Herself to be there to catch me in case I fall backwards off the seat when I jump into the car. She usually succeeds, but if I do fall I relax so that I do not hurt myself. Sometimes in London I get breathless in the street. "We'll go and see the publisher who published Rufus' life", Herself said one day. "They might publish yours too". But the walk was a little too far and that was the first time we had to rest on the way home. By the end of that winter, (by which time I was nearly 15 years of age) I was taking pills for my heart and it was necessary to stop and rest when going to the grass by the river in the afternoon. For the first time I was finding the stress and bustle of London life a little trying and when we were walking in the park I took a short cut back to the car as - in his old age - Rufus used to do to his field when we were out riding.

Like older people older dogs do not like learning anything new. "You can't teach an old dog new tricks" they say, and I will tell you a story which illustrates this. I cannot remember whether I told you how much I used to enjoy visiting the Post Office near our London home. There was a notice saying No Dogs, but I was so popular that no one minded. Everyone, particularly the children in the long queue for the counter, spoke to me. One day, however, Herself had to fill in a form and she went over to the shelf to which pens are attached."Sit and wait", she said to me, "and keep my place in the queue". I did what I was told. I did not move and soon there was a long

gap in front and more and more people queuing behind. When Herself had finished she returned and said, "What a clever dog.

Now you must learn to move up in the queue". Everybody laughed and said the same thing and when we got home she said proudly to the hall porter, "Sherry kept my place in the queue, but there was a big space in front and lots of people queuing up behind. Now we must teach her to move up in the queue".

It was the end of the sentence I did not like. What did she mean? I had done everything I was told and apparently that was not enough. Now I had to learn something new. Well, I was not going to. I was too old. So, although I had friends in the Post Office who were always pleased to see me, I made up my mind that I was not going back. It was a few days before we needed to post anything and then Herself was very surprised to find that she had to tow me in on the lead resisting all the way. "I can't make it out", she said to a friend, "suddenly she won't go near the Post Office. She does not even want to go the pillar box outside the door". It never seemed to dawn on her that it might be her fault. She did not remember the occasion of the golf ball when I did not like being told off for doing what I had been taught to do and how as a result I stopped retrieving. Now, although I had been complimented on my behaviour, I had also been told I must learn something new and I did not want to do this. Eventually we came to an arrangement. I was never asked to go into the Post Office again, but if we were going to the church gardens, which were behind the Post Office, I would not go on strike about posting letters on the way. Otherwise I would stay in the car and Herself would post them on her own.

We had another worry that spring, just before we set off for the north. We had gone away as we often did for the week-end, but because there were major road works and delays on our usual route, Herself decided with police advice to go a different way. It was an incredible journey. We crawled along behind lorries, buses and cars, changing gear. "We've taken half an hour to go 4½ miles", Herself said, thumping the steering wheel in her frustration, "that's an average speed of 9 m.p.h. It would be quicker with a horse and cart". "You must not go that way again", said our hosts when we arrived. "Yes. It used to be all right, but not now".

A few days later Herself received a disturbing communication. "I've been photographed speeding at 43 m.p.h.", she said to a friend, "but I'm sure it will be all right because I bought petrol when I set out, so I have proof that for half an hour before I was photographed I averaged 9 miles an hour!". "Go and see where the camera is before you reply", the friend replied. We had to wait nearly two weeks before taking her advice, because Herself was limping on a painful left hip, caused by constant gear changing on that crowded road. When she was better we found the camera and Herself wrote a letter setting out the facts. The next day we returned to Scotland and this time I was really pleased to go. When - five hours into the journey - we left the main road and set off over the hills I sat up and took notice. Even a glimpse of those southern hills made me feel better. Perhaps it was something to do with getting old - I wanted to get back to the hills of home and concentrate on the sights and smells that mattered.

Little did I think that, unlike previous summers when everything was happy, this one was to be fraught with anxiety. The troubles that lay in wait were caused by constant heavy rain and flooding. As soon as we were home Herself went to collect Jo from Ken and Anne, who look after him in the winter. It was too far for me to go now so she left me in the car. Jo must miss the old mare with whom he spends the winter, but he never shows it or forgets that this is his home and he is always pleased to see me. A few days later it started to rain heavily, as if buckets of water were poured from the sky. Herself was worried that morning, because she received a further communication from the police and she said to Mr. Rennie, "I've got to decide immediately whether I will go and defend this charge in London or pay. The prosecution know I averaged 9 miles an hour for $4\frac{1}{2}$ miles, and was on dual carriageway, which usually has a 40 mile an hour limit, but although I was in a line of cars in the photograph they will not let me see it or tell me if the other drivers were prosecuted." The last day to post the cheque was this first day of the torrential rain and Herself spent the morning on the telephone to police and advisers. By the time she decided to pay, the water was coming up over our side road and when we got to the bridge on the main road the river had broken its banks and was a swirling torrent. Nevertheless we got through to the Post Office and back again.

The moment we got home Herself got Jo into the stable. He is funny about wet weather. He takes the line that because it was like this in Shetland he does not need shelter. Even inside the stable he carries on with this act, saying he won't be dried and going round and round making everything as difficult as possible. The following day it rained from dawn to dusk and Jo stayed in his box. When Herself put him out next morning she said to Mr. Rennie, "Funny. There are very few droppings in the straw and he's drunk almost no water. I hope he is all right". Because the river had come up over its banks into his field she put him out into the adjoining one and because she was worried watched him carefully. At the start of the second day she saw him lying stretched out in a unusual position. When she got him up and started leading him he kept stopping and straining. She rang the vet who came and poured liquid paraffin up one nostril in a long tube into his stomach. Poor Jo. He looked utterly miserable. Then in the afternoon we went off to get a sack of bran to give him another dose. But Jo had never seen bran before and since he was feeling so unwell he thought the bran mash looked too suspicious to eat.

Later in the afternoon Herself began to be very anxious and called the vets again. Another young vet came and gave Jo more liquid paraffin, pouring it up the other nostril. Jo looked even more miserable. I had never seen him like that before, he's usually so bouncy. "I think it's something to do with the rain", Herself said to the vet, "but a chill would not show these symptoms". The vet looked at the hay and, pronouncing it excellent, agreed it was a mystery, the only unusual circumstance being the exceptionally heavy rain. After he had gone, Anne, who is the owner of Nick and very fond of Jo, came down in her landrover. By this time I could see Herself

was really worried. Probably we were both remembering Rufus' end and how in the morning he was rolled over on his back with his legs in the air. "I think we've lost him", Herself said to Anne, "he's not in any griping pain, so its not colic. But he's got the shakes all over his shoulders and down his front legs. And he's just standing utterly dejected with his head going lower and lower. He has drunk nothing and neither of the doses are having any effect. I think he's had it". But Anne came out of the stable and said, "I don't agree. He's eaten a piece of carrot". I remembered that Rufus ate a biscuit just to be polite, and that did not stop him from being dead by morning. But Anne was right. When morning came there were lots of droppings, although many were abnormally stuck together, and Jo had at last drunk some water. It seemed everything was going to be all right.

The vets remained uncertain as to the cause of Jo's illness. Two out of three were convinced it had something to do with the rain and the floods. But what? Little did anyone think there was going to be a repeat performance, so they did not delve further into the mystery for the moment. By now the rain was causing further problems which took our attention. The garage roof was leaking. "It's not worth paying for a new roof", said the builder who always has our interests at heart, "unless you get an insecticide firm to come and spray the wood to kill the wood worm". Spray! The very word sent Herself into a wheel spin. "Once bitten, twice shy", she said, "this time we'll have the best". So along came the leading insecticide firm, who said, "Our sprays don't smell at all, they are odourless". "I've heard that before", Herself replied, but this time it was true. There was no smell at all. "Keep the dog out though for 24 hours", said the operator, "as well as yourselves". Herself could regulate me and herself, but Mr. Rennie disappeared inside to get a tool. She followed him in and insisted he came out at once, but sure enough he became giddy in the afternoon, although he quickly recovered. Then the builder came and put on a new roof, stacking up the old corrugated iron sheets, which we planned to use down by the river as protection against flooding. Only Mr. Rennie expected more rain and advised pressing on with the work. No one else realised how urgent the matter had become.

CHAPTER XIV

Finishing a Task

Every day that autumn it rained and everywhere there was mud. Sometimes the rain fell in monsoon cascades, sometimes in mists of fine drops. Nevertheless the burn at the bottom of the field had not broken its banks again. On days that Mr. Rennie came to help he worked most of the time on flood defences at the burnside, where he nailed the corrugated iron sheets from the garage roof on to the fence posts, with Herself helping him with lighter work and offering advice. From time to time they harnessed Jo to the cart and built a soil bank on the inside of the fence to make a second barrier against the water and hide the ugly iron sheets from view. Old age was catching up with me now and I was becoming more breathless, so I was always given the choice, "Would you like to come down or would you like to sit in the car?" Sometimes I chose the car, sometimes the river. Then one day the car failed to start, and garage men came and towed it away. "Possibly the damp has affected the electrics", they said and later they rang to tell us that, although they could not find the cause, the car had started of its own accord, so they would bring it back again. "If it's the electrics", they warned, "you'll have to renew all main parts".

Before a decision could be made, the car failed to start again. This time the family were staying with the grandchildren, and we were going for a picnic in their Landrover over the hills to the Lonach Gathering, where pipers walk round an arena once a year playing bagpipes. The loud high notes affect my ears, so I sit under the wooden seats to muffle the noise. The car was towed away again and we piled into the family Landrover, but we never got further than the petrol station, where water flowed from the engine, so we returned home and rang the garage. "Bring the Landrover down", they said, "the car has started of its own accord again so you can go in that. It'll get you to the Games if you don't let it stop. If it doesn't start afterwards the AA will tow you home". No sooner had the family departed than the car wanted water all the time – as if there was not enough coming from the sky. So Herself carried bottles and we stopped and filled the radiator frequently. 'What you need is glue", someone said, so she bought gluey stuff in a can and poured it into the radiator. That stopped the trouble until one day we went so fast that the engine got hot and the glue melted. "This won't do", Herself said, "the car is 14 years old and has done 150,000 miles. I will buy another one". So off she went on a train, leaving me with Mr. and Mrs. Rennie, and came back with a new blue car with shiny seats, which were not as comfortable as the old ones, but it ran silently and I decided I would get used to it.

The old car sat in the garage. No one wanted it except me. It had been my kennel for so long that I could not bear to be parted from it. What were we to do now? The local garage did not want it, nor the dealer who had sold us the new car. We could not even get an offer in the sale rings, where I was driven round among cars more beautiful and younger than ours which no one wanted either. So Herself rang the garage where the Lonach Gathering was held - after all it was our car that got us there - and sold it to a young mechanic, who arrived late one evening with pounds in his pocket and drove it away. "You can fit new parts yourself", Herself said and two weeks later she was told it was going, "Like a Rolls". Is anything ever going to go right for us again, I thought. After all I am older than that car and feeling my age, but unlike it I cannot get spare parts. But perhaps these crises coming so fast upon one another were a good thing in that no one had too much time for me, because there is no cure for old age. You just have to suffer it and keep up with people and events as best you can. Herself was always reassuring. When I tumbled over sideways she came immediately and helped me to my feet saying "There you are, now you're better again. All is well", and sure enough off I would go and it would not happen again for a week or two. And if I got breathless and could not continue walking, even on the flat, then we just waited as if we had all the time in the world. I could see that she was getting older too because if we sat down after lunch and I went to sleep dreaming about happy days it was almost always me who woke up first and had to wake her and say it was time to get on. She had never gone to sleep in her chair before this year, but we had never had so much work and anxiety as we had now, all of it brought on by the rain.

Meanwhile Mr. Rennie and Herself continued to work down by the burn to make certain the water did not get into Jo's field again. Soon the corrugated iron barricade stretched right along from the copse on the hill to the snowberry hedge, where the river bank was firmer and through which no water had yet come. By now the garden rubbish that they carried down in Jo's cart had substantially increased the height of the bank, its base having been deposited a year before by our neighbour's mechanical digger, when he kindly made a path round the outside of the field, along which Jo could pull his cart without having to bump over mole hills. But as they were congratulating themselves on the success of their work, disaster struck again. Jo was stung twice in quick succession by a hornet. Suddenly with no warning he leapt into the air, almost lifting the cart off the ground. After the first sting they managed to quieten him, but the second time he went really mad, knocked Herself over with one shaft and banged the wheel on the other side against Mr. Rennie's ribs after he too was flung to the ground. If Mr. Rennie had not hung on to the reins the cart would have been smashed to bits. They could not think what had caused Jo's fright and Herself went down to the spot three times hoping to find out. On her third trip a huge hornet came fluttering by. "We'll have to find the nest," she said to Mr. Rennie when he was better. "The experts say it will be in the line of fir trees on the other side of the burn, but their only interest in the story is hearing of hornets so far north".

Now, as the work moved to completion, everyone thought we had an impregnable fortress to keep the water out. Suddenly, however, the monsoon rain started again one afternoon, with large drops coming from a black sky. We were going off to stay with friends for the night. I knew this because Herself had packed a suitcase. "I'm meant to be going to a concert of fiddle music", said Herself to Mrs. Cheyne, who had come to help clean the house, "but I think I'll ring and cancel". "You should go", Mrs. Cheyne replied, "you can't always be at the mercy of the weather and the animals. Wouldn't Mr. Rennie put Jo out if you bring him in before you go?". So that was arranged and off we went, but all the way the driving rain got worse and the cattle and sheep in the fields huddled together, utterly drenched and miserable. By the time we got home next morning Mr. Rennie had put Jo out an hour before. Sure enough the flood defences had held, but there were tiny fingers of water beginning to seep through the snowberry hedge further down the burn, where the the water had never come in before. After half an hour, therefore, Herself fetched Jo in, keeping him in all day to dry off and, after fencing off the part of the field by the snowberry hedge, putting him out for a little while in the evening and bringing him in again for the night. I could see she was in an undecided mood, not knowing for certain what had caused his illness before. "Was it water", she said to Anne on the telephone, "as you and I and two of the vets suspected or could it, as the other vet thought, have been something to do with too much standing still and eating dry food? Shetlands are a law unto themselves".

Everyone's efforts to do the right thing were in vain. Two nights later there was only one dropping in Jo's box and he had drunk no water and was starting to strain. The vet came again and poured liquid paraffin into his stomach. Still nothing happened and anxiety began to mount. The young man came twice more and poured more liquid paraffin up his nose through the tube. Jo stood all day looking hopelessly and sadly dejected and staring at the bucket of water in the corner. He could not or would not drink. Herself decided to take him for little walks every half hour and we went out on to the road to persuade him to graze where the grass was succulent but drier. Then in desperation she took him on to the lawn to let him eat the young grass shoots there. This was a place where he was never allowed to go, because his small feet sank into the soft soil. I could see him thinking, "This is extraordinary. Everyone is always so angry if I get on the lawn by mistake". Indeed in the early days I used to think he escaped on to the lawn just to annoy people. Now each time we went back into the stable he put his head into the bucket as if he wanted to drink and shook it about."That's the first and most typical sign of grass sickness," the Shetland pony breeders down the road said to Herself. "They do that but they will not or cannot drink". But I could see that Jo was thinking, "Goodness they must love me a lot to take me on their beloved lawn. I'd better make an effort to get better". And I thought when he took his head out of the bucket that perhaps he could have drunk a little. Suddenly a moment or two later he took a step forward and drank a mouthful. And then another mouthful. I could see Herself relax, she knew then that he was going to be all right.

By morning the liquid paraffin had worked and the rain had stopped. Jo was fenced off with the electric fence from the small section of grass where the water had seeped through in rivulets, and also from any part where there were pools of rain water lying. The theory of his trouble being caused by too much dry food was proved wrong. It was evident to all that the problem lay with the rain and flooding. "The vets agree with my idea of writing to the Veterinary College", Herself said to Mr. Rennie, "I'll send them specimens of grass and weeds where the flood water has left a film of muddy clay and ask them if this has been a mild form of grass sickness". When the answer came back she said to the vets who had saved Jo's life, "The College says it is sand colic, and that drinking a tiny drop of water that comes down in that burn when it is in flood, or eating a little grass with clay stuck to it, creates a sticky substance in a horse's inside. It is strange they call it colic, because Jo's symptoms started with the straining. If there were colic pains they must have been very slight. Anyway we know now for certain what causes the problem. It is drinking flood water and eating flooded grass".

Soon a friendly expert kindly came to advise us on how to keep the water out permanently. His dog was as old as me, so it stayed in the car, but I liked to oversee what was happening and I could still follow Herself down and get back up the slope if I went slowly. His advice was to continue the corrugated iron sheets right along through the snowberry hedge and to strengthen all the posts at their backs with wooden struts to resist the force of the water. This was done and because the bank itself was eroding Mr. Rennie decided it would be wise to make a breakwater of boulders, stakes and cement to stop the

soil under the fence from being threatened. By now it was November and the weather was bitterly cold. I could see that Herself was in pain because she was swathing her face in scarves. "I've got a tooth abscess on top of everything else", she said to Mr. Rennie to explain her discomfort. Because an icy wind had got up as well, I was left in the new car and when Herself went out to saw wood in the stable she took my basket with her so that I could sit in it and keep warm. All the time Mr. Rennie, although sympathetic to both our needs, was working unremittingly on the flood fortifications and I could see that Herself was wondering if it was really necessary to do all this work at this time of year – surely, surely, surely there could not be yet another flood so soon. But she kept on helping him all the same and sure enough, he was right. A third flood came within days of completion – the worst of the three. This time the defences in the big field held completely and even the cement and boulder breakwater survived very nearly intact.

Herself congratulated Mr. Rennie. "You've carried out Francis Drake's prayer, it is not the beginning of a task that is the important thing, but the continuing of it until it is thoroughly finished". But she spoke too soon. As we had seen before water is a persistent enemy and if it cannot penetrate one place it moves further down stream and comes in at another. This time the ditch leading off the burn, which divides us from the farm, had backed up with water and now it was making a little lake on our adjoining field, with pools further up the slope, all of which could be dangerous to drink. Clearly work would have to wait for the spring, but I wondered if I would be there to see it because in human terms, as Herself proudly tells people, I am 108 years of age, twenty seven years older than Mr. Rennie and thirty three years older than Herself. I'm beginning to feel that, like the old car, it is indeed a lot of years and what I want now is not more work and worry but a comfortable plateau of peace on which I can sleep and dream my own dreams.

Epilogue

Shortly after we had finished our work by the river the box in the corner of the sitting room failed to emit its proper sounds or pictures, and a man from the television company came to try and make it work properly. Afterwards he drank tea with us in the kitchen. "I met a gamekeeper", he said to Herself, "when I was doing a survey up a remote glen. He had 5 Springers with him which, he said, were all rejects from the oil rigs. Apparently the oil companies fly them out to search for drugs, and before going they receive intensive training like the police and rescue dogs – many of which are Springers – who find explosives and victims of disaster. He took on the failures and tried to train them as gun dogs, but some are so excitable that it is difficult to find homes for them. Once trained, they are intelligent and devoted, but a few are too easily distracted and find it hard to concentrate on the task in hand".

A night or two later I had a succession of dreams, as dogs often do. In the first I saw a Springer Spaniel puppy in my bed, it was almost the same colouring and markings as myself. Its head was liver, with a white liver-speckled nose and a white ruff round its neck which ran up to a V behind its head, just as mine does, and then extended down its back until it ran into a liver saddle and more liver markings on its rump. Then I woke and slept again and this time I saw it in the garden running in wild circles, leaping back and forth over the dirty drain pond in the lawn where Herself told me repeatedly not to drink. It was being very naughty, stealing tools from Mr. Rennie and Herself and running off with them to play 'catch me if you can'. This will never do I thought, they will be annoyed, as Sandy and Herself were with me when occasionally I interfered with whatever they were doing. This time when I woke I asked

myself what puppy could this be. I never had a litter, so I knew it was not mine. Where could it have come from? Before I could answer the question I dreamt again and this time I saw the puppy in the London flat, jumping on Herself's knee to watch the pigeons and aeroplanes pass the window, following her from room to room when she got up to fetch something, sleeping beside her feet so that she could not get up without rousing it first. Then I saw it in Hyde Park, not running free as I had done but on a long rope like a horse's lunging rein, to prevent it running off like a bolting horse, crossing and recrossing the main street under the cars. Once it even leapt into the Serpentine and started swimming towards the middle. Good gracious, I thought on waking, would it ever settle down and be a help and not a hindrance.

My dreams made me worry. I'll keep an eye on Herself, I thought, as long as I can, but every day I become more frail, and following her upstairs at home, which she tells me not to do, is more and more of an effort. "Stay there, I'm coming back", she says, and if I go my heart nearly bursts with the strain of climbing steps. When I am gone who will guard her, and see that she gets up early to do her writing, stops to eat meals at proper times and goes for walks? Before I could find an answer I dozed off again and saw the puppy pushing its ball under the tallboy in the London flat, using its paw to make certain it rolled out of reach. Then it fetched Herself and lay down in front of the tallboy saying with its eyes, "Please, can you help. By mistake I've lost my ball. It's under there, beyond my reach. Could you get it out please". How often had I done that! It was a wonderful way to get attention and prove that you had formed a partnership. But partnerships I thought require give and take on both sides. I hoped the puppy would learn that soon and start to listen to what it was being told.

I have heard it said that Labradors are born half-trained and Springers are born untrained. Whether this is true or false it is certainly the case that there are only a few years between the time when a dog grows up and when it starts to age, for our lives are shorter than those of the human beings we serve. The time will come when they must go on without us. One day inevitably there will be an empty basket, an empty room, an empty house, in which although our shadow is still everywhere it is now only as a ghost. Yet despite this we know that if or when another dog comes our memories will still hang in the air, bringing back recollections of close companionship and faithful friendship and proving the truth of the saying, 'When we are gone the love we gave will linger on'.